D1590756

ATTEMPT AT A
CRITIQUE OF ALL REVELATION

ATTEMPT AT A
CRITIQUE OF ALL REVELATION

By

JOHANN GOTTLIEB FICHTE

Translated, with an Introduction, by

GARRETT GREEN

Associate Professor of Religious Studies
Connecticut College

CAMBRIDGE UNIVERSITY PRESS

Cambridge
London   New York   Melbourne

Published by the Syndics of the Cambridge University Press
The Pitt Building, Trumpington Street, Cambridge CB2 1RP
Bentley House, 200 Euston Road, London NW1 2DB
32 East 57th Street, New York, NY 10022, USA
296 Beaconsfield Parade, Middle Park, Melbourne 3206, Australia

First published 1978

Printed in Great Britain by
Western Printing Services Ltd, Bristol

Library of Congress Cataloguing in Publication Data
Fichte, Johann Gottlieb, 1762–1814
Attempt at a critique of all revelation.
Translated of Versuch einer Kritik aller
Offenbarung.
Bibliography: p.181
Includes index.
1. Revelation.   I. Title.
B2833.E5 1977   231'.74   77-77756
ISBN 0–521–21707–5

Contents

Translator's Preface

This translation, to my knowledge the first ever, is based on the text of the second edition of *Versuch einer Kritik aller Offenbarung*, originally published in Königsberg in 1793. The German text is most readily available in vol. 5 of *Johann Gottlieb Fichte's sämmtliche Werke*, edited by I. H. Fichte (Berlin, 1845–6), which has recently been reissued in a photographic reprint edition in soft cover (Berlin: Walter de Gruyter & Co., 1971). The pagination of this edition is given in square brackets at the right-hand margin at the beginning of each original page. I. H. Fichte generally followed the text of the second edition; the few exceptions are indicated in footnotes.

A critical edition of the German text of the first edition (Königsberg, 1792), together with the changes and additions in the second edition, is included in the *J. G. Fichte-Gesamtausgabe der Bayerischen Akademie der Wissenschaften*, edited by Reinhard Lauth and Hans Jacob (Stuttgart–Bad Cannstatt: Friedrich Frommann Verlag [Günther Holzboog], 1962–), vol. 1, 1, pp. 3–162. Inclusive page references to this edition are provided in footnotes at the beginning of each chapter.

Major changes in the second edition are indicated in footnotes. No attempt has been made, however, to indicate the many minor changes – punctuation, stylistic alteration of occasional words and phrases, changes of emphasis – that Fichte made in the second edition; scholars interested in these changes should consult the *Gesamtausgabe*. A few brief passages omitted in the second edition are translated in footnotes, and six longer ones are translated in the Appendix (pp. 173–8 below).

The translation deliberately endeavors to render Fichte's German as literally and precisely as possible, even though some stylistic elegance in English is thereby sacrificed. As any reader of Fichte can testify, his prose is often cumbersome and unnecessarily complex, and I have resisted the temptation to improve it in the translation.

I believe that this procedure is appropriate to a technical philosophical text of this kind, which does not make for easy reading in any language. I have also tried to remain consistent wherever possible with the established tradition of English translation of German philosophy. Such consistency is especially important in this text, which makes considerable use of the technical vocabulary of the Kantian critical philosophy. I have been guided in particular by the excellent and widely-used translations of Kant's *Critique of Pure Reason* by Norman Kemp Smith and of the *Critique of Practical Reason* by Lewis White Beck. I have tried to employ the same English term each time for the corresponding German technical term. I have deviated from this equivalency only in cases where the German terms seem plainly to be employed in nontechnical senses or where clarity in English demands exceptions. Fichte's main technical terms are listed together with their English equivalents in the Glossary (pp. 179–80 below). I have also avoided the cumbersome practice of giving the original German or clarifying English emendations in the text; the few exceptions are indicated by square brackets.

I would like to thank Professors Rita S. Terras and Janis V. L. Gellinek of the Connecticut College German Department, who read some of the most difficult passages and offered valuable suggestions for improving the translation. Dr Michael Welker and Professor Klaus Hartmann of Tübingen University gave me expert advice in revising the translation. For the final result, of course, I assume full responsibility. I would like also to thank Professors Robert Horn and Hans W. Frei for first introducing me to Fichte's religious thought, Mrs Joan F. McLaughlin for typing the manuscript, Connecticut College for contributing to the cost of editorial assistance, and the Alexander von Humboldt Foundation for fellowship support during the final revision. My wife, Priscilla Green, deserves credit for stylistic improvements in the Introduction as well as personal support during the tedious process of translating.

GARRETT GREEN

Tübingen, January 1977

Introduction

The closing years of the eighteenth century and the beginning of the nineteenth were among the most exciting and creative periods of German intellectual life. It was the age of Goethe and Schiller and of the budding Romantic movement: Novalis, the Schlegel brothers, Hölderlin, and others. In philosophy the developments were no less spectacular, especially in the years spanning the publication of Kant's *Critique of Pure Reason* (1781) and Hegel's last major publication, *The Philosophy of Right* (1821). And in theology the work of F. D. E. Schleiermacher established a new direction that would dominate the religious thought of the next century and a half.

Compared to many of his contemporaries, Johann Gottlieb Fichte (1762–1814) has remained a relatively unknown figure to the English-speaking world. Only in 1970 did his major work of philosophy, the *Wissenschaftslehre*, become available in a competent English translation.[1] His name has been familiar primarily to students of philosophy as a station on the road from Kant to Hegel and to students of European history as a formative influence in the emergence of German national consciousness. His contribution to modern religious thought has been represented in English only by a popular work he wrote in 1800, *The Vocation of Man*.[2]

Quite as much as the other philosophers of German Idealism, however, Fichte played an important role in the upheaval of religious thought that accompanied the end of the Enlightenment in Europe. Emanuel Hirsch is even willing to claim that 'he belongs more than any other German philosopher in the history of Christianity and theology.'[3] Fichte's concern with religious issues was apparent from the earliest stages of his career. Like both

---

[1] *Fichte: Science of Knowledge* (*Wissenschaftslehre*), ed. and trans. Peter Heath and John Lachs (New York: Appleton-Century-Crofts, 1970).

[2] Ed. Roderick M. Chisholm (Indianapolis: Bobbs-Merrill Co., 1956).

[3] Emanuel Hirsch, *Geschichte der neuern evangelischen Theologie*, 5 vols. (Gütersloh: C. Bertelsmann Verlag, 1949–54), vol. 4, p. 337.

Schelling and Hegel, the other leading Idealist philosophers, he began as a student of theology, though his subsequent career earned him a reputation primarily as a philosopher. He was eighteen years old when he enrolled as a theological student at the University of Jena in 1780. Neither there nor in his subsequent studies at Wittenberg and Leipzig did he devote himself to a study of Kant's philosophy, the crowning works of which were coming into print during these years. Rather, he seems to have become convinced of the truth of determinism, especially as articulated in Spinoza's *Ethics*. The struggle to free himself from a deterministic view of the world began during his student years and remained a major motive throughout his subsequent life and writings.

Fichte's early Spinozism came to an abrupt end in 1790 when he finally encountered the philosophy of Kant, an experience that is appropriately described as a conversion.[4] Financial hardship had forced him to break off his studies and work for a time as a private tutor in Zurich. When he returned to Leipzig, he began an intensive study of Kant at the behest of a student who sought philosophical instruction from him. 'I am living in a new world,' he wrote to an old school friend, 'since I read the *Critique of Practical Reason*. Propositions that I believed were irrefutable have been refuted for me; things that I believed could never be proved to me have been proved to me' – and he adds, as a specific example, 'the concept of an absolute freedom.' He admits that he began his study of the *Critique of Pure Reason* 'out of necessity,' but after discovering Kant's second *Critique* he was motivated by 'real relish.' He perceived in the Kantian practical reason not only a power to renew philosophy but 'a blessing for an age in which morality has been destroyed down to its very foundations.'[5] It proved also to be a power that changed the course of his own life and set the agenda for his contribution to philosophy.

[4] Nicolai Hartmann, *Die Philosophie des deutschen Idealismus*, 2nd ed., 2 vols. in 1 (Berlin: Walter de Gruyter & Co., 1960), vol. 1, p. 42.
[5] J. G. *Fichte-Gesamtausgabe der Bayerischen Akademie der Wissenschaften*, ed. Reinhard Lauth and Hans Jacob (Stuttgart-Bad Cannstatt: Friedrich Frommann Verlag [Günther Holzboog], 1962–) (hereafter cited as *Gesamtausgabe*), vol. III,1, *Briefwechsel 1775–1793*, pp. 167–8.

I

The story of the composition and publication of Fichte's *Attempt at a Critique of All Revelation* is one of the most fascinating in the history of modern thought. It is the story of a struggling and impoverished young scholar, his pilgrimage as a devoted disciple to meet the great master, and the case of mistaken identity that launched his career as a famous philosopher.

The spring following his conversion to Kantian philosophy, Fichte accepted an opportunity to travel to Warsaw to work as a private tutor for the son of a noble family. But a disagreement with his employer ended the relationship almost as soon as it began, and Fichte, declining offers to find him another position in Poland, decided to use his severance pay to go to Königsberg and study philosophy at the feet of the master.

Frustrated in his initial attempts to attract Kant's attention and lacking an introduction, Fichte soon hit upon a plan: he would make his own letter of recommendation by writing a 'critique of revelation' dedicated to Kant. He began writing in mid-July, shortly after his arrival in Königsberg, and on 18 August he finished the manuscript and sent it, bearing the dedication 'To the Philosopher,' to Kant along with an obsequious covering letter. The ploy worked, for when Fichte called on Kant five days later to hear his response, he was graciously received. Kant, however, admitted having read only the first few pages and sent Fichte off with the suggestion that he study further in the *Critique of Pure Reason* with the help of Kant's friend, the court chaplain Schultz.[6]

Fichte's relationship with Kant might have ended here had not another set of circumstances intervened. Ten days after visiting Kant, Fichte calculated that he had money enough remaining to subsist only for another two weeks. He resolved to reveal his financial plight only to Kant, but when he thought of going to see him his courage failed. A few anxious days later Fichte summoned the courage to write an elaborate letter to Kant asking him for a loan of the necessary funds for the return journey to Saxony and offering only 'my honor in pledge.'[7] The next day Kant replied that he had not yet made up his mind. But three days later he again summoned Fichte and made an unexpected proposal: that Fichte

---

[6] Ibid., vol. II, I, *Nachgelassene Schriften 1780–1791*, p. 415.
[7] Ibid., vol. III,I, pp. 260–4.

sell his manuscript for publication to Kant's own publisher. When Fichte spoke of revising it, Kant replied that it was 'well written' – though it is clear that he had still read only a small part of it.[8] Negotiations with the publisher proceeded slowly; but in the meantime Chaplain Schultz, supported by a recommendation from Kant, obtained a position for Fichte as private tutor for a noble family in Krockow, a town near Danzig in West Prussia. Free at last from financial hardship, Fichte went to Krockow in October 1791, leaving an intermediary in Königsberg to work out the details of publication.

While Fichte waited impatiently for news about the progress of his manuscript, another unexpected crisis developed. According to Prussian law of 1788, publications on religious topics were required to pass the censorship of the theological faculty in Halle, then under the leadership of a particularly orthodox dean. After months of waiting, Fichte finally learned from Schultz at the end of January 1792 that permission to publish the *Critique of All Revelation* had been denied. The controversial points seem to have been primarily the questions of whether a given revelation could rationally be based on belief in miracles and whether the subject matter as well as the form of a revelation could extend our knowledge of dogmatic and moral matters. Schultz advised Fichte to tone down some of the more offensive passages, but Fichte chose instead to turn to Kant for advice. He summarized his position on the controversial issues in a letter to Kant and insisted that he could see no reason for changing what he had written, but he asked Kant to confirm this conclusion. He also expressed his outrage that the theological faculty could presume to pass judgment on a philosophical treatise of this kind. Kant, though acknowledging that he still had not read the complete manuscript, privately supported Fichte's refusal to alter his conclusions – though he refused to have his name implicated even indirectly. Encouraged by this expression of support from his mentor, Fichte finally decided to make no changes in the manuscript. '. . .I am now resolved,' he wrote to Kant in February 1792, 'to leave the essay as it is and to leave it to the publisher to do with it as he will.'[9]

---

8 Ibid., vol. II,1, p. 418. As late as May 1793, Kant acknowledges in a letter to Fichte that he still has not read Fichte's *Critique* in its entirety (ibid., vol. III,1, p. 408).

9 Ibid., vol. I,1, *Werke 1791–1794*, p. 9; vol. III,1, pp. 284–9, 297.

What the publisher did with it proved to be a surprise to everyone. Revisions turned out to be unnecessary in any case, for in the meantime there was a new dean at Halle who decided to allow the book to be published in its original form. The *Attempt at a Critique of All Revelation* made its debut at the Easter Fair in Leipzig in 1792 before Fichte had even seen a copy. The first copies, however, had some strange omissions: although the title, publisher, city, and date appeared in their customary place on the title page, neither Fichte's name nor his signed preface were included. No one has ever accounted for these omissions conclusively. When the second edition appeared the following year, the publisher appended a footnote to the 'Preface to the First Edition': 'Through an oversight, this preface and the genuine title page signed by the author were omitted in the Easter Fair edition but issued later.' Since, however, not only the author's name on the title page was omitted but also his preface – the only part of the text that made reference to the personal circumstances of the author – it is reasonable to conclude that the omissions were not 'an oversight' at all but rather 'a speculation by the publisher,' in the words of an editor of Fichte's collected works.[10]

If the omissions were in fact due to the publisher's 'speculation,' it was certainly a successful one. Many readers, including the first reviewers, assumed that Kant was the author. The philosophical method, the terminology (including *Critique* in the title), and the publisher all pointed to Kant, especially since he had been widely expected to write a treatise on religion. Even the anonymity of the book led some to conclude that Kant was fearful of clashing with the strict Prussian censorship. The most respected scholarly journal of the day, the *Allgemeine Literatur-Zeitung* in Jena, first called attention to the book as obviously authored by Kant and then published a lengthy and laudatory review. Kant was provoked to publish a formal announcement in a subsequent issue, in which he identified the true author, calling him a 'skillful man,' and disclaimed any part in the book in order to 'leave the honor for it undiminished to the one to whom it is due.'[11]

While the events of the summer of 1792 quickly established his reputation as an important philosopher, Fichte in his rural isolation

---

[10] Fritz Medicus, introduction to vol. 1 of Joh. Gottl. Fichte, *Werke: Auswahl in sechs Bänden* (Leipzig: Fritz Eckardt Verlag, 1911), p. xliv.

[11] *Gesamtausgabe*, vol. 1,1, pp. 10–12.

only learned of them later. Still apparently rather bewildered several months later, he wrote to his fiancée:

Why did I have to have such utterly strange, excellent, unheard-of good luck? Others, who certainly did not come forward with any less talent, were buried under the great flood and had to struggle through half their lives just to be noticed. I was elevated at the first appearance by a propitious, unforeseen, incalculable event.[12]

But Fichte wasted little time in bewilderment. Even before the public discussion about his book had reached its climax, the publisher was urging him to prepare a second edition.[13]

Fichte had begun to rework his *Critique* only a few days after delivering the original manuscript to Kant. About the same time, however, his financial plight became critical, and Kant's judgment that the manuscript was suitable for immediate publication ended any possibility of an early revision. By the time that the book's initial success created a demand for a second edition, Fichte's ambitions had already turned towards more grandiose projects. Had he the leisure, he wrote in September 1792, he would like 'so to speak to retract it completely and to put in its place a more extensive work.'[14] Unable to carry out this plan in so short a time, he added a 'Theory of the Will' (§2) at the beginning and a few less extensive passages here and there in the remaining chapters. Otherwise, the only changes were minor revisions of diction and style, which were completed by late winter in 1793. This second and final edition of the *Attempt at a Critique of All Revelation* appeared in Leipzig at the Jubilate Fair that spring.

The story of Fichte's first work culminates in his appointment the following year to the chair of philosophy at Jena vacated by the Kantian philosopher K. L. Reinhold – who, appropriately enough, was one of those who had taken Kant to be the author of the *Critique of All Revelation*.

II

It is a safe guess that more people are acquainted with the story *about* Fichte's first book than are familiar with the arguments it contains. Most accounts of his intellectual development, even those

[12] Ibid., vol. III,1, pp. 403–4.
[13] Ibid., p. 348.　　　[14] Ibid., p. 341.

which concentrate on his religious views, begin with the *Wissen-schaftslehre* of 1794.[15] To be sure, an argument can be made in support of this procedure, since Fichte's *Critique of All Revelation* shows him still under the dominant influence of Kant; he has not yet discovered the basic principle of the absolute ego, which signals his fundamental transformation of Kant's critical philosophy into an idealist system. Nevertheless, Fichte's treatise on revelation is significant for at least two reasons. First, it is the earliest attempt to apply the conclusions of the critical philosophy specifically to religion, anticipating Kant's own *Religion within the Limits of Reason Alone* by more than a year. It is therefore a useful companion piece to Kant's book, whose distinctive views on religion emerge all the more clearly from the comparison. Second, Fichte's *Critique* is interesting in the context of his own subsequent development. Before turning to the latter issue, however, it will be useful to review the course of Fichte's argument, especially in comparison with Kant's philosophy of religion.

The widespread assumption that the originally anonymous treatise was the work of Kant, of course, is a clear indication of Fichte's philosophical presuppositions. The *Attempt at a Critique of All Revelation*, in fact, seems in many respects to be more 'Kantian' than Kant's own subsequent treatment of religion. Fichte takes for granted the conclusions already worked out in Kant's three *Critiques*. The immediate point of departure for Fichte's work is the *Critique of Practical Reason* (though elements of the *Critique of Judgment* can also be detected), in which the location of religion on the map of man's rational faculties had already been indicated. Having shown the entire realm of the supernatural to be off limits for human knowledge in the *Critique of Pure Reason*, Kant devoted his second *Critique* to reclaiming much of this theoretically forbidden territory in the name of 'practical' reason, which in the Kantian lexicon is equivalent to 'moral' reason. In particular, the notions of God's existence and of the immortality of the soul are now provided with a firm rational status as 'postulates' of practical reason, even though theoretical knowledge of their truth continues to be impossible. Rational man's experience as a moral agent, standing under

---

[15] Two notable exceptions to this practice are Frederick Copleston, *A History of Philosophy* (London: Burns and Oates, 1963), vol. 7, pp. 76–8; and Wolfgang Ritzel, *Fitches Religionsphilosaphie* (Stuttgart: W. Kohlhammer Verlag, 1956), pp. 39–63.

the absolute authority of the moral law, requires that he assume, or 'postulate,' these two ideas. Kant's practical *Critique* had also indicated, though only in passing, the definition of religion as 'the cognition of all duties as divine commands,'[16] a position that he later elaborated in *Religion within the Limits of Reason Alone*.

In order to see what Fichte does on the basis of these fundamental religious propositions in the critical philosophy, it will be useful to look closely at his analysis of three central concepts: *God, religion*, and finally – the concept towards which the entire treatise is directed – *revelation*.

Fichte, like Kant, approaches the analysis of religion from the starting-point of morality – in other words, from practical reason alone. Kant's dictum that 'morality leads inevitably to religion'[17] is equally appropriate to Fichte's position. The first step beyond morality in the direction of religion is accomplished by postulating the existence of God. In Kant's practical *Critique* this step is taken rather simply by noting first that the implied object of the will acting morally is the highest good. This concept includes not only perfect virtue, the fulfillment of every command of the moral law, but also the perfect happiness of one who so wills. In other words, the object of the moral law, the highest good, ideally combines virtue and the happiness proportional to it. Morality, however, belongs wholly to the realm of freedom (practical reason) while the requirement of happiness involves events in the realm of nature (theoretical reason). In order for the highest good to be possible, therefore, it is necessary to assume (postulate) God, a supreme being who is the cause not only of the moral law but also of the natural law and who can therefore insure the ultimate coincidence of virtue and happiness.[18]

Fichte's version of this argument is essentially equivalent to Kant's, though he works it out in somewhat different conceptual terms and in greater detail, especially in the second edition of the *Critique of All Revelation*, where he includes an elaborate 'Theory of the Will' (§2). According to his argument, the first step towards a concept of God is the recognition that the sensuous impulse has a

16 Immanuel Kant, *Critique of Practical Reason*, trans. Lewis White Beck, The Library of Liberal Arts, vol. 52 (New York: Liberal Arts Press, 1956), p. 134.
17 Kant, *Religion within the Limits of Reason Alone*, trans. Theodore M. Greene and Hoyt H. Hudson (New York: Harper & Row, Harper Torchbooks, 1960), p. 7n.; see also p. 5.
18 Kant, *Critique of Practical Reason*, pp. 4, 114–17, 128–30.

right to whatever is not forbidden by the moral law. Situations can arise, however, in which such a right must subsequently be rescinded. For example, every man has the right to life, but he may in a special instance be required by morality to sacrifice his life on behalf of some higher good. Unless the moral law is to contradict itself (and thus become irrational, which is impossible), it must be possible to conceive of an ultimate goal in which there will be 'a perfect congruency of the fortunes of rational beings with their moral dispositions' (p. 60 below), that is, a situation in which the right to happiness of one who acts morally is finally vindicated. Here Fichte arrives at the same point as Kant. For this ultimate right must not merely be conceivable for practical reason; it must also be effective in the natural world. For this purpose there must necessarily exist 'a being who determines nature entirely by self-activity, in whom moral necessity and absolute physical freedom are united' (p. 60). God, then, in Fichte's most concise definition, is 'that being who determines nature in conformity with the moral law' (pp. 119–20).

A significant feature of the philosophy of religion of both Kant and Fichte is the fact that the concept of God logically precedes that of religion. In fact, the idea of God functions as a kind of pivot, a point of transition in the 'inevitable' movement of thought from morality to religion. Although the postulate of God's existence belongs to the province of practical reason, it does not in the strictest sense constitute a part of ethics. Kant, especially, is concerned to avoid any appearance that the idea of God is necessary to support morality. Fichte, as we will see, is less consistent on this point; but in order to understand what is at stake in this issue, one must examine their views on religion.

Faith is the term employed by both Kant and Fichte to designate the rational assumption of the postulates of practical reason.[19] The German word (*Glaube*), especially in the eighteenth century, did not carry connotations of nonrational subjective experience and might well be translated 'belief.' The two philosophers, of course, intended a certain ambiguity in the word, since it describes both a religious act and a philosophical concept. Such rational faith, however, is not equivalent to religion. But at this point the views of Fichte and Kant must be treated separately.

The concept of God together with his attributes, which can like-

[19] Ibid., p. 130.

wise be postulated on the basis of practical principles, Fichte designates collectively as a *theology*, a term not used in this way by Kant. Theology is constituted by the body of (practical) truths which we must necessarily assume 'in order not to set our theoretical convictions and our practical determination of the will in contradiction' (p. 63). But now Fichte introduces an important distinction: theology, which is 'mere science, dead information without practical influence,' is to be distinguished from *religion*, which must have a causal influence in determining the will to obey the moral law (p. 63). Assuming the derivation of *religion* from *religare*, Fichte concludes that it must be 'something that *binds* us,' something that contains a power to aid the will in obeying the moral law.

In the most difficult – and most original – portion of his treatise, Fichte now seeks to answer the question, 'how then does religion arise out of theology?' (p. 63). He is forced to struggle with a fundamental dilemma implicit in the Kantian equation of morality and religion. On the one hand, morality must be autonomous in order to be morality; reason cannot be answerable to any external law but must derive the rules for right thinking and willing from its own nature. The content of divine law, therefore, must be identical with the moral law of reason. As far as morality is concerned, it makes no difference 'whether we consider ourselves obligated to something because our reason commands it or because God commands it' (p. 70). But the concept of divine law then appears to be utterly superfluous. Religion, which by definition must have a binding causal influence on our moral will, therefore seems to be impossible. How can religion introduce anything new into the situation without thereby threatening the autonomy of the moral law?

Fichte's solution to this dilemma depends on a distinction between the form and the content of God's will. There can be no contradiction between morality and religion as long as their content remains the same. Kant's equation of moral duties and divine commands asserts precisely this material identity. Fichte continues to hold open the possibility, however, of a formal distinction between the moral law as known immediately through practical reason and the will of God. If the latter is not to be heteronomous, it must be 'based on an alienation' of our subjective obligation to obey the moral law in the form of 'a being outside us,' namely, the idea of God. This alienation (*Entäusserung*) turns out to be the fundamental religious principle (p. 73). Up to this point, however, Fichte is still unable to show that this representation of the authority of the moral law as the will of God makes any difference.

The final step in Fichte's transition from theology to religion is the most precarious one. He must insist that the idea of God's will can in no way increase our respect for the moral law. But he nevertheless argues that 'in particular cases,' where one experiences a strong inclination to ignore moral commands, the idea of the divine will can 'add a new gravity to the commandment of reason' (p. 74). He comes perilously close to outright contradiction at this point, but he endeavors to show that even while reason respects the moral law the additional idea of divine authority is able to inject an extra motivation to convert this respect into concrete moral acts. This latter factor, of course, answers to the definition of religion.

The question still remains concerning the relationship between the internal and external laws, the moral within and the idea of the divine lawgiver without. Since it is morally impossible to conceive God to be the cause of the specific content of the moral law, he must be conceived to be 'the cause of *the existence of the moral law in us*' (p. 75). The question of how this causality is to be conceived leads directly to the concept of revelation. The problem is now posed for the deduction of revelation itself: 'We have to seek a principle from which God's will would be recognized as the ground of the existence of the moral law in us' (p. 75).

Fichte's systematic search for a causal relationship between the will of God and the existence of the moral law in human beings leads to a further distinction within the idea of religion, which he designates by the usual Enlightenment terms, natural and revealed. His way of making the distinction, however, departs from the usual procedure. Religion, he has already shown, is the proclamation by God of the moral law as his will. But such a proclamation might take place either internally, in our rational nature, or externally, through an empirical occurrence in the natural world. The first case would be called natural religion, and Fichte argues that such a proclamation does in fact take place. We already know by practical reason that God is the supreme causal agent in nature – or, in traditional terms, creator of the world. We know also that he is 'executor of the moral law' and therefore wills the final purpose of the moral law, namely, that we as moral beings ultimately attain both perfect morality and happiness. As human beings, we are related to God according to both these realms; that is, we are creatures in the natural world as well as moral beings. The content of the moral law, of course, is known by reason and does not depend on natural causality. However, Fichte argues, our *consciousness of* the moral law does depend on nature, since 'our self-consciousness stands completely under natural laws' (p. 78). Therefore, he concludes, our very consciousness of the moral law is itself a divine proclamation of that law, since God is the author of our nature. This recognition of the 'supernatural in us' is what Fichte calls natural religion (pp. 76–8).

Only by means of this complex conceptual analysis does Fichte finally arrive at the concept to which the critique is directed: revelation. Beginning from the foundation of Kantian ethics, he proceeded to the concept of God, which led in turn to theology, religion, and revelation.

Religion, as Fichte has shown, is the appropriate name for God's proclamation of his will by means of our immediate consciousness of the moral law. This internal 'proclamation,' however, is the concept of natural religion and should not be confused with revelation, which would properly designate a divine proclamation outside us, that is, in the world of sense (p. 78). Revealed religion would have to be based on 'a fact in the sensuous world,' which could be immediately perceived as an action of God. A critique of revelation has the task of investigating the possibility of such an occurrence and bringing systematic order and clarity to its concept. The central task of the book, therefore, is to investigate the rational possibility of a revelation, understood to be 'the concept of an appearance effected in the sensuous world by the causality of God, through which he proclaims himself as moral lawgiver' (p. 96).

However much this task may appear to require a search in the external world for a datum corresponding to the concept of a revelation, Fichte's commitment to the critical philosophy clearly precludes this option. For this procedure would be a classic example of confusing theoretical and practical principles, since it would seek a supernatural object in the natural world. In order to eliminate the possibility of such an error, Fichte again introduces a distinction between form and matter. Revelation, briefly stated, is a way of making something known. Its content is simply that which is made known, and its form is 'the way in which it is made known' (p. 82). Clearly, a *formal* investigation of revelation would fall into the impossible dilemma of seeking the supernatural in the world of nature, a point which he made in a single paragraph in the first edition but expanded into an entire chapter (§5) in the second. There is simply no way for rational creatures to know theoretically whether God proclaims his will in the external world.

Fichte has now narrowed the search for a tenable concept of revelation down to a single possibility: namely, to approach it through its content by means of practical reason. It has already been established, however, that the material of a revelation must be identical with the moral law. Therefore, the appropriate question can be stated as follows: Can we conceive of a situation in which God, as postulated a priori by practical reason, would find it necessary to proclaim the moral law to be his will by means of an appearance in the sensuous world? If grounds for such an assumption can be demonstrated, then Fichte will have established the rational possibility of acknowledging an occurrence to be a revelation of God. Such a demonstration would be a priori, since it would be deduced from pure practical principles without regard for any particular datum of experience; but it would amount to a demonstration only of the *possibility* of a revelation (p. 92). The concept of revelation, therefore, cannot claim the status of the postulates of practical reason (such as the existence of God), which are necessarily to be assumed by all rational beings. All Fichte's critique claims to do is to establish the possibility that an individual might properly include such a concept as an idea of reason. He is saying, in effect: if there is indeed a revelation (something that cannot be known), this is necessarily the way we must conceive it.

After so long and complicated a preparation, the actual 'deduction of the concept of revelation,' takes place in a single long paragraph (pp. 95–6). Since human beings stand under the dual laws of nature and of morality, a struggle is inevitable between their sensuous nature and their rational obligation to will the moral law. If it should happen that there are some men in whom the natural law has so overpowered the moral law that they are affected only by sensuous causality, then obviously they can be induced to obey the moral law only if it is presented to them 'by way of the senses' (p. 95). Since God is obliged to advance morality in any way possible, then his only recourse would be to proclaim himself through a special appearance in the world of sense, designed expressly for this purpose and for these men. 'Since God is determined by the moral law to promote the highest possible morality in all rational beings by every moral means,' Fichte concludes, 'it is to be expected, if such beings should really exist, that he would avail himself of this means if it is physically possible' (p. 96).

From this focal point of the critique, the remaining tasks follow almost automatically. The first and most important of them is to demonstrate as persuasively as possible that a state of moral corruption is likely to occur sufficient to require the extreme measure of a divine revelation in order to awaken moral sensitivities (§8). Fichte then faces the difficult task of explaining how an event in the natural order, which appeals to the senses, can be the ground for rational obedience to the moral law. The idea seems to be contradictory, since genuine morality must spring autonomously from one's own free will but any external motivation for behavior would result in moral heteronomy. He tries to get around this difficulty by claiming that the external authority of revelation is not intended to ground obedience but only 'attention to the motives for obedience, which are to be displayed subsequently' (p. 111). This device is reminiscent of the man in the old joke who claimed that his mule was not stubborn at all as soon as he got his attention by hitting him over the head with a hefty stick. The success of this argument depends on Fichte's assumption that men who are originally motivated to moral behavior for the wrong reasons may progress to the point where they are eventually able to grasp the purely rational grounds of the moral law and even to apply these rational criteria to the original revelation.

The remaining task of the treatise is the working out of these specific 'criteria of the divinity of a revelation.' They contain no surprises, since they amount simply to a reassertion in detail of the requirement that a revelation adhere to the canons of practical reason. An occurrence that conforms to all of the criteria *may* be a revelation, since its content has been shown to be identical with morality. Since the question of the 'form' of the revelation – that is, the way in which it is communicated in the natural world – has already been declared to be transcendent and therefore beyond the scope of reason, no higher degree of certainty is possible. One is never rationally justified in making the judgment that a given appearance *is* a revelation; even after it has been shown to meet all the 'criteria', one is justified only in concluding, 'that *may* be revelation' (p. 151).

If Kant had published no further views on religion, Fichte's *Critique of All Revelation* might reasonably be assumed to have articulated the religious implications of Kant's philosophy. It appears to be based quite solidly on the foundation of the three Kantian *Critiques*. In fact, however, Kant was already at work on his own philosophy of religion while Fichte's manuscript awaited the imprimatur of the government censor. His essay on radical evil in human nature, which subsequently became book one of *Religion within the Limits of Reason Alone*, appeared as an article in April 1792, and the entire book was published the following year. It is an exceedingly complex work, strangely lacking in the architectonic consistency of his *Critiques*. The orderly procedure of Fichte's work gives it the appearance, at least, of closer kinship to Kant's major writings. The contents of Kant's *Religion*, however, offer a richer and broader treatment of religion, even if presented in a confusing manner.

Not surprisingly, there is a wide area of agreement between Fichte and Kant about the philosophical analysis of religion. For this very reason, however, the few striking differences between them are especially interesting and revealing of each author's point of view.

The most surprising feature of Kant's philosophy of religion, especially for an eighteenth-century thinker who considered himself to be an advocate of Enlightenment, is his assertion of radical evil in human nature – a view that he explicitly identifies with the traditional Christian doctrine of original sin.[20] His reinterpretation of this doctrine becomes the point of departure for his explication of religion, since it expresses the problem to which religion purports to be the solution. Kant reaffirms the traditional emphasis of Western Christianity on the fundamental bias towards sin in human nature, which he describes as a 'propensity to evil.'[21] He does not, however, share the Augustinian doctrine of the bondage of the will. However inconsistently, Kant affirms both an inexplicable tendency to moral evil in human beings and an equally inexplicable moral freedom to will the good nevertheless. The fundamental religious problem is how man can overcome the radical evil of his inclinations and achieve his destiny of perfect fulfillment of the moral law. Sin, therefore, is the necessary precondition of religion.

[20] Kant, *Religion*, p. 26.
[21] Ibid., p. 23.

Though in a much more muted form, Fichte's description of religion contains a corresponding feature in the 'empirical datum' that must be presupposed if revelation is to be a rational possibility. Only if it can be shown that there are human beings in whom sensibility has so overpowered morality that it has completely lost its ability to influence their actions, is revelation thinkable. Even in natural religion, Fichte finds it necessary to demonstrate the possibility that in certain cases human beings may choose to ignore the clear voice of conscience unless it is reinforced by the idea of God's will. Here, as in Kant's doctrine of radical evil, sin is the precondition for religion. In the case of Fichte, however, the evil is not so radical; the man who does not need the religious representation of the divine will in order to follow his conscience is deserving of 'a far greater admiration' (p. 74). Revelation, he states explicitly, is 'not for human beings in general, but only for those sensuous human beings who need such a presentation' (p. 144). Because Kant acknowledges the universality of sin, he also recognizes a universal need for religion.

What appears merely as a difference of emphasis between the two philosophers in their doctrines of sin becomes a clear contrast in their views on the church. Kant's greatest concession to 'positive' religion (religion in its historical and social manifestations as contrasted with the 'natural' religion of pure moral reason) is contained in his idea of the 'ethical commonwealth.' Because all men are inclined to evil actions, human society tends to reinforce the worst aspects of its individual members. In order to counteract this social power of evil, men of good will must band together into a society of mutual support in the struggle for the moral improvement of the race.

Fichte's concept of religion, by contrast, contains no doctrine of the church at all. The arena of the moral struggle is the individual will, what Fichte calls the faculty of desire. Nowhere in his *Critique of All Revelation* does he show any particular concern for the social dimensions of either sin or religion. He claims at the end of his treatise to have secured the rights of individuals to acknowledge a revelation or not as they please. Fichte's greater optimism about man's ability to act morally without external support apparently precludes any doctrine of the church. Rather, the concept in Fichte's account that comes closest to serving the practical function of Kant's ethical commonwealth is revelation itself. For it is faith in a concrete revelation of God's will that provides the extra incentive to follow the moral law for those whose moral condition is desperate enough to require it.

But in the final analysis Kant no more than Fichte is comfortable with religious positivity. Religion grows out of ethics, and ethics in turn out of reason; all aspects of religion, therefore, must finally be held accountable before the court of reason. Even the church, along with other positive elements of religion, is finally acceptable only provisionally; the positive 'vehicle' will ultimately pass away leaving only pure rational faith.[22] Fichte, too, foresees an ultimate withering away of positive religion. 'Under the guidance of a wise revelation that is in wise hands,' he writes, the means for furthering morality ought 'more and more to give up their admixture of crude sensibility, because this ought to become more and more dispensable' (p. 145). Thus even the carefully proscribed conception of a rationally acceptable revelation is finally only a stopgap measure.

The agreement of Kant and Fichte that true religion must conform fully to requirements of rational morality leads to a common problem in their philosophy of religion. Both want to demonstrate that morality leads to religion; but both want also to show that religion is something unique in its own right and not simply another name for morality. This aim, however, competes with the ethical requirement that moral actions must be autonomous. How can religion introduce anything new into the ethical situation of man without thereby introducing an element of heteronomy that undermines the morality it is supposed to fulfill?

Fichte and Kant are fully in agreement about the moral content of religious faith. As soon as they attempt to explain how it is that religion goes beyond ethics, however, a subtle but important difference appears in their views of religion. Fichte defines religion as 'something that *binds* us' more strongly than we would be bound by the moral law proclaimed inwardly by reason. However carefully he tries to hedge this idea around with moral safeguards, it remains clear that religion provides a supplementary incentive to moral obedience. It is just this key step, however, that Kant refuses to take in his *Religion*. 'For its own sake,' he emphasizes at the very start, 'morality does not need religion at all.' Unfortunately, Kant is not entirely consistent in this emphasis, for he is later able to describe certain religious representations as 'incentives' to moral

[22] For example, ibid., p. 126n.

behavior.[23] But his more predominant and consistent argument is that religion serves the purpose of bringing conceptual clarity to the final purpose of morality. His crucial analysis of justification by faith 'has done no more than answer a speculative question'; it is not, however, unimportant, since it protects reason from the charge that its moral expectations are irrational.[24] In summary, then, religion is a supplementary moral incentive in Fichte's *Critique of All Revelation*, while in Kant's *Religion within the Limits of Reason Alone* it provides reason with a coherent account of its ultimate moral expectations.

III

It is difficult to believe that the author of the *Wissenschaftslehre*, or *Science of Knowledge*, of 1794 is the same man who had written the *Attempt at a Critique of All Revelation* such a short time before. Perhaps the apparent discontinuity between the two works is one reason why Fichte's first publication is so often ignored. The subsequent changes in his philosophical position appear easy to explain compared with the 'illuminating flash of lightning' that changed the direction of his thinking in 1793.[25] His son and editor of his collected works, I. H. Fichte, saw in the *Critique of All Revelation* 'nowhere a trace' of anything pointing beyond Kant's philosophy to 'the future discoverer of the principle of the identity of the subjective and objective.'[26] It is tempting to look to Fichte's marriage in 1793 for an explanation of the dramatic turn, but even if this were possible it would tell us little about the *philosophical* reasons for the change.[27] Fortunately, however, this turning point in Fichte's intellectual development can be explained, at least with the benefit of hindsight, without recourse to matters beyond philosophical content.

Fichte himself was plainly dissatisfied with the *Critique of All Revelation* from the very beginning. Even in the letter to Kant that

[23] Ibid., pp. 3, 63.
[24] Ibid., p. 70.
[25] Hirsch, *Geschichte der neuern evangelischen Theologie*, vol. 4, pp. 345–6.
[26] I. H. Fichte, Preface to vol. 5, *Johann Gottlieb Fichte's sämmtliche Werke*, 8 vols. (Berlin, 1845–6), p. ix.
[27] Hartmann does indulge in a little such speculation when he attributes the rapid maturing of Fichte's philosophy to 'the quiet of domestic life' (*Philosophie des deutschen Idealismus*, vol. 1, p. 42).

accompanied the original manuscript Fichte described his own work as 'poor.' It would be easy to read this remark as false humility (a frequent device in Fichte's later writings) if his subsequent remarks, private as well as public, were not so consistent in this judgment. A short time later he repeated the negative evaluation in a letter to a friend, suggesting that he had arrived 'at correct results by means of incorrect premises.' To the same friend he wrote in 1794 that 'the critique of revelation seemed very mediocre to me when I wrote it.' Other remarks as late as 1799 repeat the theme, sometimes coupling it with the excuse that only Kant's urging caused him to publish it in the first place. He expresses gratitude that the book was so well received by the public but adds that he would not have praised it so highly himself.[28]

Fichte offers some clues to the source of his dissatisfaction with the treatise on revelation when, in several of the places cited above, he links his criticism of the book with a plan to correct its shortcomings in a more comprehensive 'critique of the ideas of reflection.' In a letter written in March 1793 he states his intention to write such a critique before the following spring, and he identifies the 'ideas of reflection' explicitly as 'the concepts of providence, miracles, revelation.'[29] A short time later the second edition of the *Critique of All Revelation* appeared, in the preface of which he publicly announced his intention to write the more comprehensive critique. But what appeared instead the following year was Fichte's first version of the *Wissenschaftslehre* – a work that is surely comprehensive but does not otherwise fit the description of a 'critique of the ideas of reflection.' What can account for so surprising a change of plans in so short a time?

I. H. Fichte overlooked at least one 'trace' of his father's later idealist system in the *Critique of All Revelation*. 'We are obliged by our reason,' the elder Fichte had written in discussing the physical possibility of a revelation, 'to derive the entire system of appearances, and ultimately the entire world of sense, from a causality through freedom according to rational laws, and specifically from God's causality' (p. 120). Kant had always insisted on the primacy of practical reason, but never had he gone so far as to suggest that 'the entire system of appearances' might be derived from practical principles. Implicit in this remark is a rejection of

[28] *Gesamtausgabe*, vol. I,1, pp. 7–8; vol. III,1, pp. 254, 268–9.
[29] Ibid., vol. III,1, p. 379.

the fundamental Kantian dichotomy between theoretical and practical reason. But it is precisely this step that Fichte subsequently takes, and it marks the beginning of his idealist system – the beginning, in fact, of the movement beyond Kant's standpoint that is called German Idealism. The sentence cited – with the important exception of the final reference to 'the causality of God' – could be taken as a summary of the program that Fichte in fact carries out in the *Wissenschaftslehre* of 1794.

But the key to this radical transformation of the Kantian dualism on which the *Critique of All Revelation* takes its stand into the idealist system of the *Wissenschaftslehre* lies not in the programs that the two works try to carry out, but rather in the basic problem to which they are both addressed. This key is Fichte's lifelong struggle with determinism, which had begun even before his discovery of Kant and would continue to the end of his life. Stated positively, his basic motive was to find a philosophical justification of freedom. The opposition of freedom and necessity came to be expressed by Fichte in terms of the fundamental duality of Kant's critical philosophy. It was not the theoretical philosophy of the *Critique of Pure Reason* that first aroused Fichte's enthusiasm for Kant but rather the moral philosophy of the second *Critique*. One commentator makes the astute observation that the first *Critique* 'could not have attracted the mind of the young Fichte if he had not perceived that it was an indispensable introduction to the amazing moral philosophy which had brought about his sudden and total conversion to the Critical philosophy.'[30] Kant's practical philosophy seemed to Fichte to offer a vindication of freedom. From the very beginning, however, Fichte showed more interest than Kant himself in the problem of relating the two 'uses' of reason, and at first they seemed to converge in religion. But eventually Fichte saw that he could not do justice to Kant's principle of the priority of practical reason on the basis of Kant's own critical philosophy. It was this awareness that came upon him shortly after publication of the second edition of the *Critique of All Revelation* and led him to transform Kant's critical philosophy into a system of absolute ethical idealism.

The overriding concern of Fichte's thought from his earliest work

---

30 Herman-J. de Vleeschauwer, *The Development of Kantian Thought: The History of a Doctrine*, trans. A. R. C. Duncan (London: Thomas Nelson and Sons, 1962), p. 172.

on was to vindicate freedom and morality against the threat of determinism. Kant's dualistic philosophy seemed finally just to leave the two realms in juxtaposition, however much Kant might assert the priority of the practical. Fichte's significance in the development of German Idealism, according to Richard Kroner, is that he 'first fully subordinates the logical idea to the moral.'[31] In the *Wissenschaftslehre* of 1794, Fichte carries out this program. Abandoning the Kantian 'thing-in-itself' (*Ding an sich*), he is able to overcome the radical duality of theoretical and practical and (in the words of the *Critique of All Revelation*) 'to derive the entire... world of sense from a causality through freedom according to rational laws.' Rather than beginning philosophy with the basic Kantian duality of the experiencing self over against the world of objects, Fichte attempts to proceed only on the basis of the sheer original act of consciousness itself, which is logically prior to the intuition of any object. Instead of starting with empirical *fact*, Fichte takes his point of departure in the *act* of consciousness. This new first principle for philosophy is the concept of the 'I' (*das Ich*), usually translated as 'ego' or 'self.' It is the source of all experience, whether of sensuous objects in the world of nature or of intelligible ideas in the realm of freedom. But this idealism effectively subordinates the former to the latter; reason itself is now seen to be essentially practical. Henceforth Fichte insists that there are only two consistent systems of philosophy: idealism and 'dogmatism' (sometimes called 'realism'), which begins with the assumption of objects outside the self and leads inevitably to determinism.[32]

The achievement of this new fundamental principle accounts for the radical contrast between Fichte's work on revelation and the first version of his idealist system. In the former work Fichte, following Kant, relates theoretical and practical reason in the postulate of God. The parallel 'causalities' of nature and morality meet ultimately in the idea of God. In the *Wissenschaftslehre* Fichte in effect turns the entire procedure around and posits an original unity underlying both realms in the concept of the absolute ego or self. This is not to say, however, that the absolute ego is God; but it does fulfill the philosophical function of relating freedom and necessity,

[31] *Von Kant bis Hegel*, 2 vols. in 1 (Tübingen: J. C. B. Mohr [Paul Siebeck], 1961), vol. 1, p. 42.
[32] Heath and Lachs, Preface to *Science of Knowledge*, p. ix; Copleston, *History of Philosophy*, vol. 7, pp. 38–9.

the task previously assigned to the concept of God. On the other hand, Fichte explicitly denies that the *Wissenschaftslehre* is atheistic.[33] Nevertheless, he has little occasion to mention God in the system, for the concept has in fact become unthinkable. The idea of God, which would exclude all of the distinctions within the ego, is a philosophical absolute that functions only as a limiting concept. Since this new concept of God excludes both personality and self-consciousness, it threatens the rationalist theism of the Enlightenment as well as more orthodox Christian belief.[34]

The religious implications of Fichte's early idealism did not become the focus of attention until 1798, when a brief journal article by Fichte about the grounds of faith in a divine governance of the world touched off a storm of protest.[35] The ensuing 'atheism controversy' is an intriguing episode of censorship and academic freedom, which issued the following year in Fichte's dismissal from his chair of philosophy at Jena on the grounds that he was teaching atheism. The article that provoked the dispute in effect develops the religious implications of the *Wissenschaftslehre* by trying to base belief in a moral ordering of the world on the transcendental ego.

Fichte's identification of religion and morality remains as fundamental in the period of the atheism controversy as it had been when he wrote the *Critique of All Revelation*. The difference is that morality no longer stands opposed to a deterministic natural order but is rather implicit in the free activity of the pure ego. Morality is now identical with the element of *purpose* that is immediately present in the activity of the ego. When the ego 'posits' the sensuous world, it does so in accordance with its inherent purpose – that is, in accordance with morality. The world, in fact, is by definition 'the material of our duty made sensuous.' In other words, the very order of the world *is* precisely its moral order. Faith in the reality of such a world, ordered according to moral principles, is what Fichte can now call revelation. What occasioned the charge of atheism was

[33] *Science of Knowledge*, p. 245 n.4.
[34] Copleston, *History of Philosophy*, vol. 7, pp. 78–80; Hirsch, *Geschichte der neuern evangelischen Theologie*, vol. 4, p. 352.
[35] 'Ueber den Grund unseres Glaubens an eine göttliche Weltregierung,' in *Sämmtliche Werke*, ed. I. H. Fichte, vol. 5, pp. 177–89; 'On the Foundation of Our Belief in a Divine Government of the Universe,' trans. Paul Edwards, in *19th Century Philosophy*, ed. Patrick L. Gardiner (New York: The Free Press, 1969), pp. 19–26.

Fichte's insistence that this moral view of the world is equivalent to belief in a *divine* governance of the world. 'That living and working moral order is itself God,' he wrote; 'we need no other God and can conceive no other.'[36]

That Fichte did not intend to present an atheistic philosophy is quite certain; whether he may have done so inadvertently depends on what kind of 'theism' one accepts. (Schleiermacher suggested that Fichte should ask his opponents for the legally sanctioned definition of God's existence in the German Empire.)[37] Fichte did deny the personality and self-consciousness of God, and this alone would be sufficient to arouse the ire of both churchmen and proponents of Enlightened natural religion. The most accurate label for his position is probably pantheism, since he denies that 'God' designates any reality beyond or behind the world.[38] This new conception of God and his relationship to the world is the most striking change in Fichte's philosophy of religion from the *Critique of All Revelation* to the period of the atheism controversy.

The story of Fichte's intellectual development after 1794 is the story of the *Wissenschaftslehre*, which he continued to expand, revise, and develop for the rest of his life. The details of this development would shed little light on the *Attempt at a Critique of All Revelation*, but the overall tendency of Fichte's later thought bears a significant relationship to the concerns of his first work. For ironically, beginning about the time of the atheism controversy, Fichte's philosophical thought moves in an increasingly religious direction.[39] Signs of this movement are present in *The Vocation of Man* (1800) and become clearly evident in the versions of his system from 1801 to 1804. He introduces the concept of pure being alongside that of consciousness; the absolute ego becomes simply the Absolute, and he can eventually speak of it as Life and Light – and finally God. The *Wissenschaftslehre* evolves in the end into a system of ethical and idealistic pantheism. In 1806 Fichte again published a book specifically on religion, in which

[36] Ibid., pp. 185, 186.
[37] Hirsch, *Geschichte der neuern evangelischen Theologie*, vol. 4, p. 359; cf. Friedrich Schleiermacher, *On Religion: Speeches to Its Cultured Despisers*, trans. John Oman (New York: Harper & Row, Harper Torchbooks, 1958), p. 93.
[38] Hartmann, *Philosophie des deutschen Idealismus*, vol. 1, p. 101.
[39] For an account of this development, see ibid., pp. 71–80; cf. Copleston, *History of Philosophy*, vol. 7, pp. 83–93.

he shows a renewed interest in relating his theory to Christian tradition.[40]

Neglect of Fichte's first work has helped to obscure the central religious motif running throughout his career. In all of the forms his ideas took, he was continually searching for the philosophical vindication of freedom that would overcome the dichotomy of necessity and freedom, theoretical reason and practical reason, nature and morality, being and thought, object and subject. In the Kantianism of his *Critique of All Revelation* the principle of ultimate unity is God. He soon abandoned this concept for a new unifying principle, the absolute ego, which eventually evolved back to a concept of God. The God of Fichte's late period is, of course, conceived in radically different terms from the God whose existence and attributes are 'deduced' in the *Critique of All Revelation*. But the attempt to place Fichte's first work in the context of his later intellectual development has brought to light his basic philosophical motive and revealed its essentially religious implications.

IV

Fichte's treatise on revelation is one of the last religious writings of the European Enlightenment. Beyond its usefulness in understanding the religious doctrines implied by Kantian critical philosophy and its importance for interpreting Fichte's intellectual development, this text is an important document of the radical transformation of religious thought that occurred at the end of the eighteenth century. Although it plainly partakes of the rationalistic spirit of *Aufklärung*, it also contains seeds of the new world of idealist and romantic religion that was soon to dominate European thought, beginning with Fichte himself. It therefore offers insight into the change between the eighteenth- and nineteenth-century intellectual worlds as well as the persistent issues that have shaped the religious thought of the modern world as a whole.

Kant's thought is commonly recognized as the great watershed of modern philosophy and theology. The critical acid of the *Critique of Pure Reason* dissolved the foundations of the Enlightenment

---

40 *Anweisungen zum seligen Leben*, in *Sämmtliche Werke*, ed. I. H. Fichte, vol. 5, pp. 397–580; *The Way Towards the Blessed Life, or The Doctrine of Religion*, trans. William Smith, in *The Popular Works of Johann Gottlieb Fichte*, 4th ed., rev. (London: Trübner & Co., 1889), vol. 2, pp. 289–496.

rationalism on which both rational orthodoxy and its Deistic opponents depended. Less frequently emphasized is the constructive correlate of this attack on the old metaphysics: namely, Kant's equally revolutionary attempt to establish a new, 'practical' foundation for metaphysical and theological assertions. Less attention has been paid by philosophers to this affirmative aspect of Kant's thought since the demise of idealist philosophy in the latter half of the nineteenth century. For religious thought, however, it remains as important as the critical revolution, as can be seen by examining the central concept in Fichte's *Critique of All Revelation.*

When Fichte decided to write his own 'letter of recommendation' to Kant, he chose as his topic the most important and controversial idea in the whole of modern religious thought. Revelation was already a central issue in the seventeenth century, and a look at the most recent writings of contemporary theologians shows that its importance continues unabated in the late twentieth century. It has persisted because it raises the most serious problems of religion in the modern era, and its very persistence makes it a useful barometer of changes in the perception of and approach to these problems over the past three centuries.

First in England and then in Germany, the eighteenth-century battle lines had been drawn between proponents of a 'natural religion,' founded on the clear and universal principles of reason and consisting wholly or primarily in the practice of moral virtue, and defenders of 'revealed religion.' One of the major causes of Enlightenment religion was the spectacular success of the new science of the seventeenth century in explaining the workings of physical nature according to mathematically rational principles. Religious rationalists claimed a corresponding clarity, universality, and authority for the tenets of 'natural' religion – natural because it, like modern physics, 'is founded on the Reason and Nature of Things.'[41] The leading Deists did not simply reject revelation. Rather, they sought to show that its genuine content was identical with that of natural religion, which in effect undercut the claim that revelation was authoritative for religion. It differs from natural religion, in the words of Matthew Tindal, only 'in the Manner of its being communicated.'[42] The consequence of this position, quite

[41] Matthew Tindal, *Christianity as Old as the Creation* (1730; reprint ed., Stuttgart-Bad Cannstatt: Friedrich Frommann Verlag [Günther Holzboog], 1967), p. 13.   [42] Ibid., p. 3.

intentional on the part of the Deists, was to make revelation and the traditional religious practices and institutions based upon it super-fluous.

So when Fichte set out in 1791 to investigate the rational basis for acknowledging a revelation, he was pursuing the leading issue of eighteenth-century religious controversy. In addition, he shared with his Enlightenment predecessors the assumption that the only legitimate content of religion is morality and that the difference between natural and revealed religion is the means by which that content is communicated. Consequently, he also encounters the problem of the apparent superfluity of revelation, which he struggles valiantly though finally unsuccessfully to overcome. In his 'Conclud-ing Remark' he claims to have established a middle position between those who would deny all revelation and those who would insist on acknowledging one as a test of true religion. In terms of the eighteenth-century debate, Fichte's position could be called moderate Deism, since he takes natural religion to be the final authority but tries to allow also for belief in revelation.

But the undeniable continuities between the Enlightenment and Fichte's analysis of religion and revelation cannot disguise the fact that he already stands on the other side of the Kantian watershed. He may still speak of a natural religion in conformity with reason, but he now understands 'reason' in a fundamentally different way. Even the most radical Deists never doubted that the propositions of natural religion were factual assertions about supernatural reality. For Fichte, as for nearly all religious thinkers since Hume and Kant, such theoretical knowledge is impossible. No longer is reason conceived as an essentially passive faculty for receiving information about reality but rather as an active process giving conceptual shape and meaning to sense data. Fichte may have agreed in the equation of morality and religion, but he, following Kant, reverses their logical order. No longer does moral obligation rest on the firm foundation of rational knowledge of God and his will; now the immediate sense of moral obligation becomes the foundation for the rational construction of such concepts as God and revelation. Already evident in Fichte's application of the new method are some of the characteristic traits of nineteenth-century religious thought.

Fichte's distinction between religion and theology, an idea that he did not learn from Kant, foreshadows one basic feature of nineteenth-century thought. For both rational orthodoxy and the Deists of the eighteenth century, religion was characteristically (though not exclusively) constituted by assent to certain propositions, whether based on reason or on revelation. The force of Kant's first *Critique*, therefore, was to cut the ground from under both sides in the debate, since both claimed 'theoretical' knowledge of supersensuous reality. Fichte's use of *religion* to apply to the 'binding' aspect of immediate moral obligation was thus a fundamental shift in the meaning of the concept. The element of rational conceptuality he called theology, but it was now understood to be based on 'practical' experience rather than on theoretical apprehension. This distinction between religion and theology thus grows out of the new dichotomy between subject and object, which became a persistent philosophical and theological problem for the nineteenth century. Here is the point at which Kant's new constructive method is so revolutionary for religious thought. Its significance is often overlooked because the specifically ethical content of the Kantian and Fichtean theology did not prove to be influential. Their basic methodological procedure, however, begins a pattern that has been repeated in countless variations ever since. Some aspect of immediate human experience (corresponding to moral obligation in Kant and Fichte) is identified with religion (often called *faith* in the nineteenth and twentieth centuries); theology is then understood to be the rational or systematic articulation of the immediate religious experience. Schleiermacher is rightly credited with establishing this new theological direction; but a crucial aspect of his methodology is anticipated in the philosophical theology of Kant and Fichte.

Fichte's concept of religion in the *Critique of All Revelation* also foreshadows the major problem inherent in the new theology of the nineteenth century. Since theological statements are no longer directly descriptive of external reality but rather of some aspect of immediate consciousness, they run the risk of appearing to be wholly subjective. 'The idea of God,' Fichte says, '. . .is. . .based on an alienation of what is ours, on translating something subjective into a being outside us. . .' (p. 73). Kant, while admitting that 'it does indeed sound dangerous,' goes so far as to say that 'every man *creates a God* for himself.'[43] When Fichte says that 'this alienation is the real *principle of religion*,' he uses almost the same language

<hr>

[43] *Religion*, p. 157n.

that Feuerbach later employs in his thesis that the 'essence of religion' lies in its illusory projection of ideal human attributes in a pseudo-subject called 'God.'[44] In attempting to avoid the atheistic consequences of Hume's skepticism and Kant's critique of rational theology, the new 'practical' theology thus sowed the seeds of the new atheism of the nineteenth century.[45] Theologians ever since have made repeated attempts to steer a course between the old dangers exposed by Kant's first *Critique* and the new dangers implicit in his second *Critique* and exposed by Feuerbach.

The long and constantly shifting debate about revelation since the seventeenth century is not only an indicator of changes in religious thought but also a clue to a persistent underlying issue. Although the rationalists of the eighteenth century, adapting terms long familiar to Western theology, frequently spoke in terms of natural and revealed religion, they did not usually conceive them to be in strict opposition to one another or mutually exclusive. The Deist controversy was not so much about whether revelation should be acknowledged as about what constituted genuine revelation. The thesis of the Deists is succinctly captured in the subtitle of Matthew Tindal's *Christianity as Old as the Creation* (1730), often called the 'Deists' Bible': *The Gospel, A Republication of the Religion of Nature*. Revelation, in other words, is perfectly acceptable so long as it conforms to 'nature.' The Deists often employed another term, *positive* religion, to identify the objectionable aspect of revealed religion, the direct antithesis to natural religion. Tindal, for example, sets himself the task of demonstrating 'how inconsistent it is with the Good of Mankind, to suppose any merely positive Things to be Part of the Ingredients which constitute True Religion.'[46] Simply stated, 'positive' elements of religion were any 'external' laws, beliefs, or practices not reducible to rational principles. However radically the ideas of reason, religion, and revelation may have changed in the closing years of the eighteenth century, an underlying polemic against religious positivity continues to be a frequent

---

44 Ludwig Feuerbach, *The Essence of Christianity*, trans. George Eliot (New York: Harper & Row, Harper Torchbooks, 1957), chap. 1.
45 See Alasdair MacIntyre, 'God and the Theologians,' *Encounter* 21, no. 3 (September 1963), pp. 3–10, and the elaboration of his two types of atheism by Hans W. Frei, 'Feuerbach and Theology,' *Journal of the American Academy of Religion* 35 (September 1967), pp. 250–6.
46 Tindal, *Christianity as Old as the Creation*, p. 140.

and characteristic feature of nineteenth-century religious thought.[47]

The issue of positivity brings out an essential feature of Fichte's argument in his *Attempt at a Critique of All Revelation*. His aim is to subject the concept of revelation to a philosophical critique, which means to reduce it to a priori principles of pure practical reason (p. 39). Implicit in this very method is the requirement that 'genuine' revelation include only rational (moral) content. The eviscerated conception of revelation that finally emerges from Fichte's critique is essentially nonpositive (or natural) revelation. According to this 'practical' concept, God may undertake 'by way of the senses' to induce men who are capable of responding only to 'sensuous causality' to obey the moral law (which, of course, is not sensuous but intelligible). This sensuous means of presenting the moral law is revelation. It is not positive because by definition it can communicate only the moral law, which is in principle available to all men through the use of their reason. It may still be called revelation because to the sense-bound creatures for whom it is intended it does reveal something (the moral law) that they would not otherwise have known.

The concern with positivity, which persists even though the term falls into disuse after the eighteenth century,[48] is also a key to the philosophical interpretation of Christianity in the modern period. Many of the major thinkers of the eighteenth and nineteenth centuries, especially Kant and Hegel, attempted restatements of Christian doctrine in harmony with the modern spirit. For them, as for Fichte, the apparent positivity of traditional Christianity constituted the greatest challenge for reinterpretation. Although explicit concern with Christianity is not pronounced in Fichte's *Critique of All Revelation*, the few allusions and direct references to it make clear his intention to present Christianity as identical with rational moral religion. The importance of this identification emerges in the explicit statement at the very end of the work (p. 172).

[47] This thesis is pursued with respect to early German Idealist thought in my Ph.D. dissertation, 'Positive Religion in the Early Philosophy of the German Idealists' (Yale University, 1971).

[48] The only major thinker to pay explicit attention to the issue of positivity at the end of the eighteenth century was Hegel, whose essays on 'The Positivity of the Christian Religion' and 'The Spirit of Christianity and Its Fate' were not published until 1907 (*On Christianity: Early Theological Writings*, trans. T. M. Knox and Richard Kroner [New York: Harper & Row, Harper Torchbooks, 1961]).

The special significance and interest in Fichte's first publication does not lie primarily in the theory of revelation that it propounds but rather in the way it perceives the underlying issues and the conceptual means it employs in the attempt to solve them. Viewed in this light, the *Attempt at a Critique of All Revelation* epitomizes the point of transition in the interpretation of religion between the pre-Kantian Enlightenment and the emerging movements of thought that were to characterize the nineteenth century.

Versuch

einer

Critik aller Offenbarung.

Königsberg 1792.

Im Verlag der Hartungschen Buchhandlung.

[Facsimile of original title page lacking Fichte's name; from
J. G. Fichte-Gesamtausgabe, vol. I,1, facing p. 16]

ATTEMPT AT A
CRITIQUE OF ALL REVELATION

To
Dr Franz Volkmar Reinhard
Chief Court Chaplain
As a pure sacrifice of the freest devotion
By the author[1]

Most honored Sir:

Not my own opinion of this writing but rather the favorable judgment of it by worthy men made me so bold as to give it that designation, so honorable to it, in this second edition.

It is no more within my province to praise your merits before the public than it would be possible for you to listen to it even from one more worthy: the greatest merit was always the most modest.

Yet even the Deity allows his rational creatures to let their feelings of devotion and love for him pour forth in words in order to satisfy the need of their overflowing hearts, and the good man will surely not deny this to his fellow man.

Therefore, you will certainly accept kindly the assurance of similar feelings flowing from the same source.

From the sincerest admirer of Your Reverence,

Johann Gottlieb Fichte

---

[1] This dedication was added in the second edition.

Preface to the First Edition[2]

This essay is called an *Attempt*, not as though one had in general to grope about blindly and feel for the ground in investigations of this kind and were unable ever to find a sure result, but rather because *I* may not yet credit myself with the maturity to set forth this sure result. In any event, this writing was not at first intended for publication; honorable men judged it kindly, and they were the ones who gave me the first notion of submitting it to the public.

Here it is. The style and wording are mine, and censure or disdain affecting these matters affect only me, and that is not much. The result is a matter of truth, and that is more. This result must be subjected to a strict, but careful and impartial, examination. I, at least, proceeded impartially.

I may have erred, and it would be a wonder if I had not. What form of reprimand I deserve is for the public to decide.

I will gratefully acknowledge every correction in whatever tone it may be couched and will counter as best I can every objection that seems to me to be contrary to the cause of truth. To it, to the truth, I solemnly devote myself upon the occasion of my first appearance in public. Without regard for party or for my own honor, I will always acknowledge as true what I consider to be true, from wherever it may come, and will never acknowledge as true what I do not consider to be true.

May the public forgive me for having spoken about myself in their presence this first and only time. This assurance may be [13] quite unimportant to them; but it was important to me for my own sake to make them witnesses to my solemn vow.

Königsberg, December 1791

2 This preface was originally omitted from the first edition (see Introduction, p. 5 above). It was printed in the second edition with the following note: 'Through an oversight this preface and the genuine title page signed by the author were omitted in the Easter Fair edition but issued later. *The Publisher.*'

Preface to the Second Edition

Even with this second edition the present writing still remains an attempt, embarrassing as it has been for me to approximate – though from a great distance – the kind opinion that a respectable portion of the public may have formed about the author. However firmly, in my opinion, the critique of revelation may stand on the foundation of practical philosophy as a separate adjacent structure, it only becomes joined to the whole structure by means of a critical investigation of the entire family to which that concept belongs, and which I would like to call the family of the ideas of reflection, and only by this means does it become inseparably united with it.

It was this critique of the ideas of reflection that I would have offered rather than a second edition of the present text if I had had sufficient leisure to accomplish more than I have actually accomplished. However, I shall proceed without delay to work on the materials gathered for this purpose, and this text will then be a further analysis of a portion of that critique which is to be treated only briefly there.

What I have added or changed in this second edition, and why – every expert, I hope, will perceive for himself. A few reminders, among which I mention with respect those in the *Göttingische gelehrte Anzeigen*,[3] caught my eye too late for me to be able to [14] take them into consideration expressly. Since, however, they do not concern my treatment as a whole but can be satisfied by a more extensive elucidation of specific results, I hope to satisfy the worthy reviewer fully in the prospective critique of the ideas of reflection.

I still owe the public a closer definition of the promise I made in the first preface to answer every objection to this critique that seems to me to be unfounded. I was able to make this promise only in this sense: to the extent that it would appear to me that truth itself, or

---

[3] A review, written by Carl Friedrich Stäudlin, appeared in two parts in the *Göttingische Anzeigen von gelehrten Sachen*, in the editions of 24 November and 1 December 1792, pp. 1873–87 and 1917–23.

its presentation, might profit by a discussion of the objections. And there seems to me to be no worthier way of achieving this purpose than by taking objections only tacitly into account in my future works, when I could not name the objector with the highest esteem – objections, that is, against what I actually assert or seem to assert, but not against what I expressly deny.

For the Jubilate Fair, 1793[4]

---

[4] The book appeared at the Easter or Jubilate Fair, one of the three annual trade fairs in Leipzig, which was also the center of the German publishing industry. The fair began officially on the third Sunday after Easter (Jubilate Sunday).

§1

Introduction[5]

It is a remarkable phenomenon, to say the least, that in the case of all nations as soon as they have raised themselves from the condition of complete savagery to sociality, the observer encounters notions of a communication between higher beings and humans, traditions of supernatural inspirations and influences of the Deity on mortals. Sometimes more crude, sometimes more refined, but nevertheless universal, he encounters the concept of *revelation*. This concept in itself seems to deserve some respect, therefore, even if only in virtue of its universality. And for a thorough philosophy it seems more fitting to trace its origin, to investigate its presumptions and warrants, and to pronounce judgment on it according to these discoveries than to relegate it directly and unexamined either to the fabrications of swindlers or to the land of dreams. If this investigation is to be philosophical, it must be undertaken from a priori principles – and specifically from those of practical reason if this concept should be related solely to religion, as is to be assumed at least at the outset. This investigation will also abstract completely from anything particular that might be possible in a given revelation; indeed, [16] it will even ignore the question of whether any revelation is given, in order generally to establish principles valid for every revelation.

One is only too easily carried away by a preconceived opinion in examining a topic that seems to have such important consequences for humanity, concerning which every one of its members has the right to vote – and by far the majority exercise it – and which is therefore either boundlessly honored or excessively despised and hated. Since this is the case, it is here doubly necessary to look only at the path that criticism prescribes, to walk straight along it without having an eventual goal in mind, and to await its verdict without putting words into its mouth.

[5] *Gesamtausgabe*, p. 18.

§2

Theory of the Will
In Preparation for a Deduction
Of Religion in General[6]

To determine oneself to produce a representation with the consciousness of one's own activity is called *volition*; the faculty of determining oneself with this consciousness of self-activity is called the *faculty of desire* (both [terms taken] in their broadest meaning). Volition is distinguished from the faculty of desire as the actual from the possible. Whether the consciousness of self-activity appearing in volition might not perhaps deceive us remains uninvestigated and undecided for the present.

The representation to be produced is either *given*, insofar namely as a representation can be given – as is presupposed from theoretical philosophy as settled and acknowledged as regards its *material* – or self-activity *produces* it even as regards its material as well, the possibility or impossibility of which we shall leave entirely aside for the time being.

I

The material of a representation, if it is not to be produced by absolute spontaneity, can be given only to receptivity, and this [17] only in sensation. For even the forms of intuition and concepts that are given a priori, insofar as they are to constitute the *material* of a representation, must be given to sensation, in this case to inner sensation. Consequently, every object of the faculty of desire to which a representation corresponds, and whose material is not produced by absolute spontaneity, stands under the conditions of sensibility and is empirical. So in this regard the faculty of desire is not capable of an a priori determination at all; whatever is to become its object must be sensed, and let itself be sensed, and the representation of the *matter* of the volition (the *material* of the representation to be produced) must have preceded every volition.

Now in the mere faculty of determining oneself through the

6 This chapter was added in the second edition. *Gesamtausgabe*, pp. 135–53.

representation of the material of a representation to produce this representation itself, however, the determination is not yet posited, just as in the possible the actual is not yet posited. The representation, in other words, is not to determine, in which case the subject would be merely passive – would *be* determined but would not *determine* itself – but rather *we* are to determine ourselves by means of the representation, which 'by means of' will become fully clear at once. Namely, there must be a *medium* that is determinable from one side by the representation, to which the subject is related merely passively, and from the other side by spontaneity, the consciousness of which is the distinguishing characteristic of all volition. And this medium we call the *impulse*.

That which affects the mind *from the one side* in sensation as merely passive is its material or matter, not its form, which is given to it by the mind through its self-activity.* The impulse is thus determinable, insofar as it involves a sensation, only by the [18] material element of this sensation, by the element that is immediately sensed in being affected.

That element in the matter of the sensation which has the character of determining the impulse we call *pleasant*; and the impulse, insofar as it is thereby determined, we call the *sensuous* impulse. We offer these explanations for the present as nothing more than explanations of terms.

Now sensation in general is divided into that of *outer* and that of *inner* sense. The first of these intuits indirectly the alterations of appearances in space; the second intuits directly in time the modifications of our mind, insofar as it is appearance. And the impulse, insofar as it involves sensations of the first kind, can be called *coarsely sensuous*; and insofar as it is determined by sensations of the second kind, it can be called *finely sensuous*. In both cases, however, the impulse is related solely to the pleasant *because* and *insofar as* it is pleasant. A presumed superiority of the latter could be based, however, on nothing more than the fact that its objects afforded *more* pleasure but not a pleasure different *in kind*. Someone who preferred to be determined by it could at most pride himself that he better understood enjoyment; and he could not prove even that to someone who assured him that he didn't take his finer

---

* This form of empirical intuition, insofar as it is empirical, is the object of the feeling of the beautiful. *Rightly understood*, this uncovers an easier way of penetrating into the field of aesthetic judgment.

enjoyments seriously at all but praised his coarser ones – since that depends on sensuous taste, which is not subject to dispute, and since all pleasant affections of inner sense may finally be traced back to pleasant outer sensations.

From the other side, if this impulse is to be determinable through spontaneity, then this determination takes place *either* according to given laws that are merely applied to the impulse by spontaneity, hence not directly by spontaneity, *or* it takes place without any laws, hence directly by absolute spontaneity.

In the first case, that faculty in us which applies given laws to given material is judgment. Consequently, it would have to be [19] judgment that determined the sensuous impulse in accordance with the laws of the understanding. Judgment cannot do this in the way that sensation does, by giving material to the impulse, for judgment gives nothing at all but only orders the given manifold under the synthetic unity.

All the above mental faculties, to be sure, provide abundant material through their transactions *for* the sensuous impulse, but they do not give it *to* the impulse; sensation gives them to it. The activity of the understanding in thought, the lofty vistas that reason opens to us, the reciprocal communication of thoughts among rational beings, and the like – these are certainly fertile sources of enjoyment. But we draw from these sources precisely as we are affected by the tickling of the palate: through sensation.

Furthermore, the manifold that it orders *for the determination of the sensuous impulse* cannot be the manifold of *one* given intuition in itself, as it must for the understanding in order to lead it to concepts for the purpose of theoretical knowledge. Thus it cannot be a determination of the material by form, because the sensuous impulse is determined by the material alone, and not at all by concepts (a remark that is very important for the theory of the faculty of desire, for by neglecting it one is led astray into the field of aesthetic judgment). Rather, [there must be] *manifold* pleasant sensations. The faculty of judgment during this transaction stands completely and simply in the service of sensibility, which supplies both manifold and standard of comparison: the understanding furnishes nothing but the rules of the system.

According to *quality*, what is to be judged is given directly by sensation. In positive terms it is *the pleasant*, which means precisely that which determines the sensuous impulse, and it is capable of no further analysis. The pleasant is pleasant because it determines the impulse, and it determines the impulse because it is pleasant. To want to investigate *why* something gives pleasure directly to sensation, and *how* it would have to be constituted in order to give [20] it pleasure, would amount to utter contradiction. For in that case it should be traced back to concepts, and hence it would give pleasure to sensation not directly but by means of a concept. In negative terms, it is the unpleasant; in limitative terms, what is indifferent for sensation.

According to *quantity*, the objects of the sensuous impulse are judged according to their extension and intension, everything according to the standard of direct sensation.

According to *relation*, where again only the pleasant is simply related to the pleasant: (1) with respect to its influence on the permanence of the faculty of sensation itself, namely, as it is presented directly by sensation; (2) with respect to its influence in generating or increasing other pleasant sensations – the causality of the pleasant on the pleasant; (3) with respect to the persistence or nonpersistence of several pleasant sensations together.

Finally, judged according to *modality*: (1) possibility – whether a sensation could be pleasant according to the standard of previous sensations of a similar kind; (2) actuality – that it is pleasant; (3) necessity of its being pleasant, whereby the impulse becomes instinct.

Through this determination of the manifold, which in sensation is merely *pleasant*, according to laws of the understanding – through this ordering of the manifold there arises the concept of *happiness* [*Glück*], the concept of a condition in which the sensing subject enjoys in accordance with rules. Thus, one pleasant sensation is disregarded and sacrificed to another of greater intension or extension; one that harms the faculty of sensation, to another one that strengthens it; one that is isolated within itself, to another one which itself becomes the cause of further pleasant sensations or tolerates and enhances many others besides itself. Finally, a merely possible enjoyment is disregarded and sacrificed to sensations which must of necessity be pleasant or which one experiences as actually pleasant. A finished system according to this outline would yield a doctrine of happiness – as it were, an arithmetic of sense-enjoyment.* [21] But it could have no general validity, since it would have merely empirical principles. Everyone would have to have his own system,

* Formerly also called *doctrine of morals*.

since everyone can judge only for himself what is pleasant or still more pleasant *to him*. These individual systems would agree only in form, but not in matter, because form is given by the necessary laws of the understanding. When the concept of happiness is determined in this way, it is quite correct that we cannot know what promotes the happiness of another – or indeed, in what we shall place our own happiness in the next hour.

If this concept of happiness [*Glück*] is extended by reason to the unconditioned and unlimited, the idea of *Happiness* [*Glückseligkeit*][7] arises, which can never be determined as universally valid, since it likewise rests solely on empirical principles. Everyone has his own doctrine of Happiness in this sense; one that is even just comparatively universal is impossible and contradictory.

With such a *merely indirect* determinability of the sensuous impulse through spontaneity, however, we still do not achieve any explanation at all of the actual determination. Even for this determinability to be possible we had tacitly to presuppose at least a faculty for *delaying* the determination of the impulse by sensation, because without this it would not even be possible to compare and subordinate the various pleasures under laws of the understanding in order to determine the will in accordance with the results of this comparison. This delaying, in other words, cannot take place through judgment at all, even in accordance with laws of the understanding; for in that case laws of the understanding would also have to be practical, which directly contradicts their nature. Accordingly, we must assume the second case stated above: that this delaying takes place *directly* through spontaneity.

Not only this delaying, however, but also the final actual [22] determination of the will cannot be completed merely through those laws. For everything that we accomplish in our minds according to those laws takes place with the feeling of necessity, which conflicts with the consciousness of self-activity that characterizes all volition. Rather, it must take place directly through spontaneity.

[7] The word *Glück* is regularly rendered by 'happiness' and *Glückseligkeit* by 'Happiness' (capitalized) in this translation. This admittedly artificial device is probably no more artificial than Fichte's own distinction between the two German terms. *Glückseligkeit* is the term that was normally used by philosophers, including Kant, and has usually been rendered in English by 'happiness.' When Fichte added §2 in the second edition, he also changed five occurrences of *Glückseligkeit* in §3 to *Glück* to conform to the newly-introduced distinction.

But one should not judge what we have said here too hastily, as
though we had made ourselves comfortable at this point and had
inferred directly from our consciousness of self-activity in volition
the actual existence of this self-activity. Indeed, this consciousness of
self-activity alone – the freedom which in itself and according to its
nature is nothing but negative (an absence of the feeling of necessity)
– not only *could* arise merely from the *un*consciousness of the real
cause that first delays and then determines; but in fact, if we were
to find no further ground for freedom, i.e., independence from the
coercion of natural law, it would *have* to arise in this way. In that
case the philosophy of Joch[8] would be the only true and consistent
one. But then there would also be no willing at all, the appearances
of it would be demonstrable delusions, thought and volition would
only apparently be different, and man would be a machine in
which representations would mesh with representations like wheels
in a clock. (There is no salvation from these consequences, derived
by conclusive logic, except by acknowledging a practical reason and,
as implied therein, its categorical imperative.)

So far, then, we have done nothing more than to analyze the
presupposed concept of a will insofar as it is to be determined by
the lower faculty of desire. We have shown, *if* there is a will, how
its determination is possible through the sensuous impulse; *that*
there is a will, however, we have so far neither wanted nor been
able to prove, nor have we pretended to prove. Such a proof might
perhaps result from investigation of the second case assumed above:
namely, that the representation to be produced by the action of the
will is produced, even according to its material, not by sensation
but by absolute spontaneity, i.e., by spontaneity with [23]
consciousness.

---

[8] Karl Ferdinand Hommel (1722–1781), professor of law and judge in
Leipzig and a leading advocate of penal reform during the German
Enlightenment, published a work in 1770 entitled *Von Belohnung und
Strafe nach türkischen Gesezen* ('On Reward and Punishment according to
Turkish Law') under the pseudonym Alexander von Joch. In this book
Hommel defends a deterministic account of the problem of freedom and
argues, in opposition to prevailing theory and practice, for a purely pro-
tective criminal law based on a deterministic doctrine. Hommel also
denied that he experienced the feeling of freedom, which he declared to be
an illusion. Cf. the Introduction to Karl Ferdinand Hommel, *Über
Belohnung und Strafe nach türkischen Gesetzen*, reprint of 2nd ed. of 1772,
ed. Heinz Holzhauer (Berlin: Erich Schmidt Verlag, 1970).

II

Everything that is bare material and can be nothing else is given by sensation; spontaneity produces only forms. The representation assumed would accordingly have to be a representation of something that is *in itself form*, and would be *material* only as the object of a representation of it – only *relatively* (in relation to this representation) – just as, for example, space and time – in themselves forms of intuition – are the material of a representation of space or time.

Forms proclaim themselves to consciousness only in their application to objects. Now the forms of intuition, of concepts, and of ideas that lie originally in pure reason are applied to their objects with the feeling of necessity. Accordingly, they proclaim themselves to consciousness *with coercion*, and *not with freedom*, and are thus called *given*, not *produced*.

Now if that form we are seeking is to proclaim itself to consciousness as one produced by absolute spontaneity (not as given coercively), it must do so in application to an object determinable by absolute spontaneity. Now the only thing that is given to our self-consciousness in such a manner is *the faculty of desire*; hence that form must be, objectively regarded, the *form of the faculty of desire*. If this form becomes the material of a representation, then the material of this representation is produced by absolute spontaneity. We do have a representation of the kind we have been seeking – but it must be the only one of its kind, because the conditions of its possibility are suited only to the faculty of desire – and the question posed has been resolved. Now it is a *fact of this consciousness* that such an original form of the faculty of desire, and an original faculty of desire itself, actually proclaims itself to consciousness in our mind by means of this form. And beyond this ultimate principle of all philosophy, the only one having universal validity, no further philosophy [24] takes place. By this fact, then, it first becomes certain *that* man has a will.

It also becomes fully clear in this context, as we mention here only in passing, how representations are possible which go beyond all experience in the world of sense – namely, that single representation whose material is not given by sensation but is rather produced by absolute spontaneity, and the ones derived from it. It further becomes clear how the *material* of these representations, which is purely spiritual in order to be able to be adopted into consciousness, would have to be determined by the *forms* given to us for objects of the sensuous world. These determinations, however, since they were necessitated not by the conditions of the thing in itself but by the conditions of our self-consciousness, must be accepted not as *objective* but only as *subjective* – but yet as *universally valid* for every discursive understanding, since they are based on the laws of pure self-consciousness. But they must not be extended any further than is required for them to be adopted into pure self-consciousness, because in that case they would lose their universal validity. It becomes clear, finally, that this transition into the realm of the supersensuous is the only one possible for finite beings.

Now (to take up again the thread of our consideration where we let it drop), insofar as the faculty of desire has its form originally determined for it, it is not first determined by a given object but rather gives itself its own object by this form; i.e., if this form becomes the object of a representation, then this representation is to be called the object of the faculty of desire. Now this representation is the idea of the *absolutely right*. In relation to the will this faculty impels one to will, simply because one wills. This remarkable faculty in us, then, is called the *higher* faculty of desire, and its character-istic difference from the *lower* faculty of desire is that no object is given to the former, which gives one to itself, while the latter must have its object given to it. The former is absolutely self-active; [25] the latter is in many respects merely passive.

But something more is yet required in order for this higher faculty of desire, which is still merely a *faculty*, to produce a *volition*, as a real *action* of the mind, hence an empirical determina-tion. Each volition, namely, regarded as an action of the mind, takes place with the consciousness of self-activity. Now that which the self-activity in this action affects cannot itself be further self-activity, at least not in this function; but rather, insofar as spontaneity affects it, it is merely passive, hence an affection. The form of will that is necessarily present a priori in the higher faculty of desire, however, can never be affected by a spontaneity given in the empirical self-consciousness, which would simply contradict its originality and its necessity. Now unless the determinability of the will in finite beings by that necessary form is to be completely given up, a medium must be exhibited, which on the one hand is pro-duced by the absolute spontaneity of that form and on the other hand is determinable by spontaneity in the empirical self-consciousness.* Insofar as it is the latter, it must be _passively_ determinable; hence it must be an _affecting of the faculty of sensation_. But insofar as it is to be produced by absolute spontaneity, in accordance with the first condition, it cannot be an affecting of receptivity by given _matter_. Consequently, since except for this one no positive affecting of the faculty of sensation can be conceived, it can by no means be a positive but only a _negative_ affecting – a suppression, a restriction of the faculty. But the faculty of sensation, insofar as it is _mere receptivity_, can be affected neither [26] positively nor negatively by spontaneity but only by something material being given. Therefore, the postulated negative determination can by no means have to do with receptivity (being in itself perhaps an obstruction or constriction of sensibility). Rather, it must be related to sensibility _insofar as it is determinable by spontaneity_ (see above), _is related to the will, and is called sensuous impulse_.

Now insofar as this determination is related back to absolute spontaneity, it is merely negative – a suppression of the presumption of the impulse to determine the will. Insofar as it is related to the sensation of this suppression, it is positive and is called the _feeling of respect_. This feeling is the point, as it were, at which the rational and the sensuous natures of finite beings flow intimately together.

In order to cast the greatest possible light on our further path, we want here in addition to reflect on this important feeling according to the moments of judgment.[9]

It is, namely, as just discussed, according to _quality_ a positive affection of inner sense which arises from the destruction of the sensuous impulse as the _sole_ impulse determining the will, hence from a restriction of it. Its _quantity_ is _conditionally determinable_, capable of degrees of intension and extension, empirically determinable essence in the relation of the forms of will to the law; _unconditioned and fully determined_, capable of no degrees of intension or extension, _absolute respect_, towards the simple idea of the law;

---

* That is to say, since finite beings possess the characteristic of being passively affected and of determining themselves by spontaneity in every expression of their activity, it may be assumed that they have intermediate faculties capable of being determined on the one hand by passivity and on the other by activity.

9 Cf. Immanuel Kant, _Critique of Pure Reason_, trans. Norman Kemp Smith (London: Macmillan; New York: St Martin's Press, 1968), pp. 106–10 (B 95–101).

unconditioned and indeterminable, finally, towards the ideal in which law and form of will are one. According to *relation,* this feeling relates itself to the *ego* as substance, either in *pure* self-consciousness (and becomes then *respect of our higher spiritual nature,* which expresses itself aesthetically in the feeling of the sublime), or in *empirical* self-consciousness (in respect of the congruency of our particular forms of will with the law – *self-satisfaction, shame before oneself*); or it relates itself to *the law* as the *ground* of our obligation (simply respect, the feeling of [27] the necessary primacy of law and of our necessary subordination to it), or to the *law* conceived *as substance* (our ideal). Finally, according to *modality,* respect is *possible* towards empirically determinable rational beings, *actual* towards the law, and *necessary* towards the Only Holy Being.

Something like *respect,* then, which we add here only by way of illustration, is certainly to be assumed in all finite beings in whom the necessary form of the faculty of desire is not yet necessarily the form of will. But in a being in whom faculty and action, thought and volition, are one, respect towards the law cannot even be conceived.

Now insofar as this feeling of respect determines the will as an empirical faculty and is in turn determinable by self-activity in volition (the purpose for which we have had to seek such a feeling in ourselves), it is called *impulse.* Since no volition is possible without *self-consciousness* (of freedom), however, it can be the impulse of an actual volition only through relationship to the *ego,* hence only in the form of *self-respect.* Now we have just said that this self-respect is either *pure,* simply respect for the dignity of mankind in ourselves, or *empirical,* satisfaction with the actual assertion of it. Upon consideration it certainly appears to be far nobler and more sublime to be determined by pure self-respect – by the simple thought that I *must* so act if I want to be a human being – than by empirical self-respect – by the thought that if I so act I will be able to be satisfied with myself as a human being. But in practice the two thoughts fuse so intimately that it must be difficult even for the most astute observer to distinguish precisely the part played by the one or the other in the determination of his will.

It becomes clear from what has been said that a completely correct maxim of morality is, Respect yourself. It has likewise become evident why nobler souls feel far more fear and awe before [28] themselves than before the might of all nature, and why they regard the applause of their own heart far higher than the praises of the whole world.

Now insofar as this self-respect is regarded as an *active* impulse, determining the will if not to actual volition nevertheless actively to inclination, it is called *moral interest*, which is either *pure* – interest in the dignity of mankind in itself – or *empirical* – interest in the dignity of mankind in our empirically determinable self. Interest, however, must necessarily be accompanied by a feeling of pleasure, and an interest actually asserted must produce empirically a feeling of pleasure; thus even empirical self-respect expresses itself as self-satisfaction. This interest certainly relates itself to the self, though not to *love* but rather to *respect* of this self, which feeling is purely moral according to its origin. If one wants to call the sensuous impulse selfish and the moral impulse unselfish, one can surely do so for explanation. But to me, at least, this nomenclature seems inopportune where it is a case of precise definition, since even the moral impulse must relate itself to the self in order to effect an actual volition; and empirical features seem superfluous where one has the transcendental ones discussed above.

However, the fact that the original necessary determination of the faculty of desire produces an interest, and indeed an interest that subjugates everything sensuous, arises out of its *categorically* lawful form, and is to be explained only on this presupposition.* Allow me to stay with this point for a moment.

Respect is first of all the marvelous feeling, expressing [29] itself no doubt in every man, which cannot be explained from his entire sensuous nature and points directly to his connection with a higher world. What is most marvelous is that this feeling, which in itself is surely discouraging to our sensibility, is accompanied by an unnameable enjoyment, completely different in kind from every sensuous pleasure and infinitely surpassing it in degree. Who,

* I would also add here in explanation that something like interest in the good applies merely to finite (i.e., empirically determinable) beings but is by no means to be predicated of the infinite. Hence, in pure philosophy, where one abstracts totally from all empirical conditions, the following proposition is to be expressed without any limitation: the good must take place simply because it is good. For beings determinable by sense, however, the proposition is to be limited as follows: the good effects interest simply because it is good, and this interest must have determined the will to produce it if the form of will is to be purely moral.

having felt intimately this enjoyment even once, would for any sensuous gratification exchange even, for example, his amazement at the roaring plunge of the falls of the Rhine; or raising his eyes to the eternal masses of ice, threatening to sink seemingly at every moment, with the exalting feeling, *I* defy your might;* or his self-confidence in the free and deliberate submission even to the mere idea of the universal, necessary law of nature, though this natural law may subjugate his inclination or his intention; or, finally, his self-confidence in the free sacrifice of what he holds dearest for the sake of duty? Why it is that the sensuous impulse on the one hand and the purely moral impulse on the other counterbalance each other in the human will could doubtless be explained by the fact that they both appear in one and the same subject. But the fact that the former is so far from putting itself on a par with the latter that it rather bows down before the mere idea of a law, and accords [30] a far more intimate enjoyment from its nonsatisfaction than from its satisfaction – this, or in a word, the categorical, the quality of the law as simply unconditioned and incapable of being conditioned – this points to our higher origin, to our spiritual descent. It is a divine spark in us, and a pledge that We are of His race. And here, then, reflection changes to wonder and awe. Standing at this point, one forgives the boldest fantasy its flight and is fully reconciled with the amiable source of all the rhapsodies of the Pythagoreans and Platonists, even if not with their emanations.

* Should we not be more intent in education on developing the feeling for the sublime? This is a way that nature herself opens to us to pass over from sensibility to morality; and in our age it is usually checked very early in us by frivolities and trinkets – and also, among other things, by theodicies and doctrines of Happiness. *Nil admirari;*[10] *omnia humana infra se posita cernere:*[11] is it not the invisible wafting of this spirit that draws us, here less, there more, to the classical writings of the ancients? What might we become, with our doubtless more developed humanitarian feelings compared with them, if we wished just in this regard to become like them? And what are we now compared with them?

10 'Marvel at nothing,' Horace, *Epistles* I.vi.1 (trans. H. Rushton Fairclough, Loeb Classical Library), citing an ideal common to many philosophers of the ancient world.

11 I have been unable to locate the exact source of this apparent citation, which likewise expresses an ideal common in the ancient world. A similar passage in Cicero refers to the ideal 'man, who thinks all human vicissitudes beneath him' ('*vir ... infra se omnia humana ducens,*' *De finibus bonorum et malorum* III.29, trans. H. Rackham, Loeb Classical Library).

And by this means, then, the obscurity would also be removed which has always made it difficult – especially for good souls, who were conscious of the most urgent interest in what is simply right – to understand the seemingly hard saying of the Critique that the good should not be related at all to our Happiness.[12] They are quite right when they persist in their self-confidence that they are indeed determined to truly good decisions only by interest; but they must look for the origin of this interest, if their decision was purely moral, not in sensuous feeling but in the legislation of pure reason. The nearest ground for determining their will, which does not determine it necessarily but does nevertheless generate an inclination, is certainly the enjoyment of the inner sense from intuiting the right. But the fact that such an intuition gives them enjoyment – the basis for this does not lie in some affecting of inner receptivity by the material of that idea, for this is utterly impossible. Rather, it lies in the necessary determination, existing a priori, of the faculty of desire as a higher faculty.

Thus I might ask someone: 'Would you, even if you did not believe in any immortality of the soul, rather sacrifice your life under a thousand torments than do wrong?' And he would answer me: 'Even under this condition I would rather die, and *for my own sake*, because a death that destroys me under unspeakable [31] torments is far more bearable than a life to be lived in the feeling of unworthiness, under shame and self-disdain.' And in so saying, insofar as he was speaking of the empirical determinative impulse of his decision, he would be completely right. But the fact that in this case he would have to disdain himself – that the prospect of such a self-disdain would be so oppressive to him that he would rather sacrifice his life than submit himself to it – he would search again in vain for the ground of this fact in sensation, from which he could not by any effort contrive something like respect or disdain.

Even this interest, however, still does not necessarily effect an actual volition; to that end an action of spontaneity in our consciousness is yet required, through which the volition is first completed as a true action of our mind. The *freedom of choice (libertas arbitrii)*, given to consciousness empirically in this function of choosing, also

12 Cf. Kant, *Critique of Practical Reason*, trans. Lewis White Beck, The Library of Liberal Arts, vol. 52 (New York: Liberal Arts Press, 1956), pp. 63–4.

occurs in a determination of the will by sensuous inclination, and does not consist merely in the faculty of choosing between determination according to the moral impulse or according to the sensuous impulse, but also in the faculty of choosing among several conflicting determinations by means of the latter (for the purpose of judging them). This freedom is indeed to be distinguished from the absolutely first expression of freedom through the practical law of reason, where freedom does not mean choice at all, since the law allows us no option but rather commands by necessity; here freedom signifies, only negatively, complete liberation from the coercion of natural necessity, so that the moral law does not depend on any grounds, as its premises, lying in the theoretical philosophy of nature and presupposes a faculty in man for determining himself independently of natural necessity. Without this absolutely first expression of freedom, the second, merely empirical expression could not be saved; it would be a mere illusion, and the first serious reflection would destroy the lovely dream in which we fancied ourselves unshackled for a moment from the chain of natural necessity.

If I am not mistaken, the confusion of these two very different [32] expressions of freedom is one of the principal reasons why one has such difficulty conceiving *moral* (not physical) *necessity*, whereby a law is supposed to command *freedom*. For if one conceives the characteristic of *choice* in the concept of freedom (a thought that many are still not able to resist), then *moral* necessity can surely not be combined with it. But this is totally out of the question in the case of the first, original expression of freedom, which is the only one by which it verifies itself in general. Reason gives itself a law through a spontaneity absolutely its own, independently of anything external; that is the only correct concept of transcendental freedom. Now this law commands necessarily and unconditionally, precisely *because* it is *law*; and here no choice, no selection among different determinations, takes place through this law, because it determines only in *one* way.

What follows is still by way of explanation. This transcendental freedom, as the exclusive character of reason insofar as it is practical, is to be attributed to every moral being, hence also to the infinite moral being. But insofar as this freedom is related to empirical conditions of finite beings, its expressions in this case are valid only under these conditions. Consequently, since freedom of choice depends on the determinability of a being by yet other laws than the law of practical reason, no freedom of choice is to be assumed in God, who is determined solely by this law, any more than respect for the law or interest in absolute right. And the philosophers who denied God freedom in this sense of the word, as conditioned by the limits of finitude, were completely correct.

This analysis, along with its primary aim of removing unperceived difficulties of a critique of revelation, has had also the secondary aim of clearing up some obscurities in the critical philosophy in general and opening a new door by which those who had hitherto been unacquainted with it or had opposed it might enter into it. Now in order that this analysis not be misunderstood and interpreted by critical philosophers themselves as degrading virtue [33] once more into the handmaid of pleasure, we shall make our thoughts still clearer by means of the following table:

Volition, the determination by self-activity to produce a representation, regarded as an *action* of the mind,

is

A.	B.	
pure,	*impure*,	
	a.	*b.*
when *representation* as well as *determination* is produced by absolute self-activity. This is possible only in a being that is solely *active* and never passive: in God.	when the *determination* but not the *representation* is produced by self-activity: in the case of determination by the sensuous impulse in finite beings.	when the *representation* but not the *determination* is produced by self-activity. But now by virtue of the concept of volition, the determination is always to be produced by self-activity; consequently, this case is conceivable only under the condition that although the actual *determination* as *action* happens by spontaneity, the *determinative impulse* is nevertheless an affection: moral

determination of the
will in finite beings
by virtue of the
impulse of self-
respect as a moral
interest.

Pure *volition* is accordingly not possible in finite beings, because volition is not a matter of pure spirit but of empirically determinable being. But a pure *faculty of desire* surely is possible, as a *faculty* which is not present in empirically determinable being but rather in pure spirit and reveals our spiritual nature by its very existence.

Furthermore, pure reason, at least so far as I have understood [34] it, has been explained no differently by its authorized interpreter among us – as might be shown by comparing this presentation with the one in the *Critique of Practical Reason*.*

III

The affecting of the impulse to Happiness by the moral law in order to stimulate respect is merely *negative* in relation to it *as* impulse to Happiness. If Happiness is placed merely in the *pleasant* (as must happen), even self-respect, far from producing Happiness, rather increases as Happiness decreases; and the more of a person's Happiness he has sacrificed to duty, the more he is able to respect himself. It is nevertheless to be expected that the moral law will also *positively* affect the impulse to Happiness, at least indirectly, even *as* impulse to Happiness, in order to bring unity to the whole man, both purely and empirically determinable. And since this law claims *primacy* in us, it must indeed be required.**

The impulse to Happiness, that is to say, is limited for the present according to rules by the moral law: I am not *permitted* to will everything to which this impulse could determine me. Through

---

* Which is said not by way of proof but κατ' ἄνθρωπον. Every assertion must stand or fall by itself. He does Kant little *honor* who has not noticed in the whole contour and execution of his writings that he would impart to us not his *letter* but rather his *spirit*; and still less does he *thank* him.
** The neglect of this part of the theory of will – namely, the development of the *positive* determination of the sensuous impulse by the moral law – leads necessarily to stoicism in the doctrine of morals (the principle of self-sufficiency) and to the denial of God and the immortality of the soul, if one is consistent.

this conformity to law, which for the present is merely negative, the impulse, which hitherto depended lawlessly and blindly on chance or on blind natural necessity, now comes under a law in general. Furthermore, the impulse becomes *positively* conformable to law (but not yet lawful) even where the law does not speak, so long [35] as this law is *solely valid* for it, precisely by the silence of the law. If I may *not* will what the moral law forbids, then I may will everything that it does *not* forbid. (Not, however: I *ought* to will it, for the law remains totally silent; that, rather, depends completely on my free choice.) This *permission* is one of those concepts that bear their origin on their face. It is, namely, manifestly conditioned by the moral law. (Natural philosophy knows only of 'can' or 'cannot,' but not of 'may.') But this concept is conditioned only negatively by the moral law and leaves positive determination solely to inclination.

What one is permitted to do because of the silence of the law is called negatively, insofar as it is related to the law, *not wrong*; and insofar as it is related to the conformity of impulse to law that thereby arises, it is called positively *a right*. To everything that is *not wrong, I have a right.**

Insofar as the law by its silence gives impulse a right, it is simply *conformable to law*; by this silence enjoyment merely becomes (morally) *possible*. This leads us to a modality for the justification of the impulse, and it allows us to expect that indirectly through the practical law the impulse may also become *lawful* – that an enjoyment may also become *actual* through the practical law. Now this last expression cannot be taken to mean that sensibility is to be affected as positively pleasant in receptivity by material given to it by the moral law, for the impossibility of this has already been sufficiently demonstrated above. The enjoyment, namely, is to be produced not *physically-*, but *morally- actually*, which unusual expression will immediately become fully clear. Such a moral actualizing of enjoyment would still have to be based on that negative determination of impulse by law. Through this determination, then, the impulse first receives a right. But now cases can occur [36] where the law revokes its justification. Thus everyone is doubtless justified in living; yet it may nevertheless become a duty to sacrifice

* A question in passing: Should the first principle of natural right be an imperative or a thesis? Should this science be played in the key of practical or of theoretical philosophy?

one's life. This revoking of justification would be a formal contradiction of the law with itself. Now the law cannot contradict itself without losing its lawful character, ceasing to be a law, and being forced to surrender itself completely.

The foregoing would lead us for the moment to conclude that all objects of sensuous impulse, in accordance with the requirement of the moral law that it not contradict itself, could only be appearances, not things in themselves, and that such a contradiction is therefore grounded in the objects insofar as they are appearances, and is thus illusory. So this proposition is just as surely a postulate of practical reason as a theorem of theoretical reason. There would accordingly be no death, no suffering, no sacrifice for duty in themselves; rather, the illusion of these things would be based merely on that which makes the things into appearances.

However, since our sensuous impulse does extend even to appearances, and since the law justifies it *as* such – hence insofar as it so extends – it cannot, therefore, revoke this justification. Hence it must, by virtue of its required primacy, have command also over the world of appearances. Now the law is not able to do this *directly*, since it applies itself *positively* only *to the thing in itself*, to our higher, purely spiritual faculty of desire. Thus it must take place *indirectly*, hence *through the sensuous impulse*, on which it of course works negatively. From this there arises, then, a positive *lawfulness* of the impulse, derived from its negative determination by the law.

From him who dies for duty, for example, the moral law takes away a previously granted right. But the law cannot do this without contradicting itself; consequently, this right is taken from him only insofar as he is appearance (here, in time). His impulse to life, justified by the law, demands back the right as appearance, hence in time, and by this legal demand becomes lawful for the world [37] of appearances. He who, on the contrary, did not sacrifice his life when required of him by the law is unworthy of life and must lose it as appearance, if the moral law is to be valid also for the world of appearances, in accordance with the causality of this law.*

From this lawfulness of the impulse arises the concept of *worthiness for happiness*, as the second moment of the modality of justification. *Worthiness* is a concept that is obviously related to morality

---

* What a strange coincidence! He who loves his life will lose it, but he who loses it will keep it for eternal life, said Jesus [cf. John 12.25] – which says precisely as much as the above.

and cannot be obtained from any natural philosophy. Furthermore, *worthy* obviously means more than a right: we admit a right to an enjoyment to many a person whom we nevertheless consider to be very unworthy of it; but conversely, we will deem no one worthy of a happiness to which he has no right originally (not even hypothetically). Finally, one also discovers in practice the negative origin of this concept, for in judging whether someone is worthy of an enjoyment, we are forced to think the actual enjoyment away.

It is one of the outward signs of the truth of the critical moral philosophy that one cannot take a single step in it without hitting upon a principle deeply imprinted in universal human sentiment – a principle that can be explained easily and intelligibly by that philosophy, and only by it. Here, then, the sanction and claim of retaliation (*jus talionis*) is a universal human sentiment. We wish for everyone that life may go for him just as he makes it for others, and that things may happen to him in accordance with his actions. Even in the commonest judgments, accordingly, we regard the appearances of his sensuous impulse as lawful for the world of appearances; we assume that his modes of conduct, in regard to himself, should be valid as universal law.

This lawfulness of impulse, then, requires the complete congruency of the fortunes of a rational being with his moral behavior, [38] as the first postulate of practical reason applying to sensuous beings. It requires that that appearance always ensue which would have had to ensue if the impulse had been determined legitimately by the moral law and had been legislative for the world of appearances.

And here, without noticing it, we have simultaneously overcome a difficulty that has not been noted, as far as I know, by any opponent of the critical philosophy, but which has therefore afflicted it none the less: namely, how it is possible to relate the moral law, which in itself is applicable only to the form of will of moral beings as such, to appearances in the world of sense – which nevertheless had to happen necessarily, for the purpose of a postulated congruency of the fortunes of moral beings with their behavior and the further rational postulates deducible from this. This applicability, namely, becomes clear solely from its lawfulness for the world of appearances, which is derived from the negative determination of the impulse to Happiness.

Finally, in the third moment of the modality, right and worthiness are conceived in combination, in which right loses its positive character as the conformity of sensuous inclination to law* and worthiness loses its negative character as having arisen through abrogation of a right by a commandment. Thus arises a concept which positively is transcendent for us because all its limits are removed by thought but which negatively is a condition in which the moral law has no sensuous inclination to limit because none exists. This concept of infinite Happiness with infinite right and worthiness** – *blessedness* – is an indeterminate idea, which is nevertheless established for us by the moral law as the ultimate goal, and which we continually approach, since the inclinations in us come ever closer to agreement with the moral law and our [39] rights should thus extend themselves further and further. But we can never reach this goal without destroying the limits of finitude. And then the concept of the entire highest good, or *blessedness*, would be deducible from the legislation of practical reason. The first part of it, *holiness*, would be deducible *purely*, from the positive determination of the higher faculty of desire by this law, which has been done so clearly in the *Critique of Practical Reason* that a repetition is unnecessary here.[18] The second part, *blessedness* (in the narrower sense), would be deducible *impurely*, from the negative determination of the lower faculty of desire by this law. But we must not be led astray by the fact that in order to deduce the second part we had to begin from empirical premises. For in part, that which was to be determined was empirical but that which determined was purely spiritual; and in part, everything empirical in the rational idea of blessedness deduced from these determinations should be conceived as nonexistent and this idea should be grasped purely spiritually, which for sensuous beings is certainly not possible.

* God has no rights, for he has no sensuous inclination.
** These last two concepts are there only to indicate the empty place of an idea which arises from their combination and is inconceivable for us.
18 Cf. Kant, *Critique of Practical Reason*, pp. 32–3.

§3

Deduction of Religion in General[14]

We deduced above, from the requirement of the moral law that it not contradict itself by abrogating its justifications of the sensuous impulse, an indirect lawfulness of this impulse itself and a perfect congruency of the fortunes of rational beings with their moral dispositions, which is thereby to be assumed. But then the impulse, even if by this means it obtains *lawful rights* as a *moral* faculty, has no *legislative power* as a *physical* faculty; rather, it is itself dependent on empirical laws of nature and must simply await its satisfaction passively from them. Accordingly, that contradiction of the moral law with itself in application to empirically determinable beings would merely be further postponed, not fundamentally cancelled. For even if the law gives the impulse a right to demand its satisfaction, this is still not sufficient for it, since it does not seek [40] merely a right but the assertion of its right, which it cannot assert itself. It remains as unsatisfied as ever, regardless of the permission of the moral law to satisfy itself. Therefore, the moral law itself must assert these rights which it bestows by itself, if it is not to contradict itself and cease to be a law; hence, even over nature it must not only command but prevail. Now it cannot do this in beings who are themselves affected passively by nature but only in a being who determines nature entirely by self-activity, in whom moral necessity and absolute physical freedom are united. Such a being we call *God*. The existence of a God is thus to be assumed just as certainly as a moral *law*: there *is* a God.

In God *only* the moral law prevails, and it does so *without any limitation*. God is *holy* and *blessed*, and when the latter is conceived in relation to the world of sense, *almighty*.

God must,[15] by virtue of the claim of the moral law upon him,

---

[14] *Gesamtausgabe*, pp. 19–36 (§2). The first two paragraphs (as far as note 15 below) were added in the second edition, replacing a longer passage in the first edition, which is translated in the Appendix, pp. 173–4 below.

[15] See note 14 above.

produce that complete congruency between the morality and the happiness of finite rational beings, since only through and in him does reason prevail over sensuous nature: he must be *totally just*.

In the concept of everything that exists in general, nothing is conceived but the series of causes and effects according to natural laws in the world of sense, and the free decisions of moral beings in the supersensuous world. God must oversee the former totally, for he must by virtue of his causality have determined the laws of nature through freedom and given the first thrust to the series of causes and effects following according to those laws. He must know all of the latter, for they determine the degree of morality of a being; and this degree is the standard by which the distribution of happiness to rational beings must take place in accordance with the moral law, whose executor he is. Since, then, nothing is conceivable [41] for us except these two instances, we must conceive God to be *omniscient*.

So long as finite beings remain finite, they will continue to stand – for that is the concept of finitude in morality – under other laws than those of reason. Consequently, they will never be able to produce by themselves the complete congruency of happiness with morality. The moral law, however, requires this quite unconditionally. Therefore, this law can never cease to be valid, since it will never be achieved; its claim can never end, since it will never be fulfilled. It is valid for eternity.

It makes this claim on that holy being: to promote eternally the highest good in all rational natures, and to establish eternally the balance between morality and happiness. That being must thus be eternal himself, to correspond to an eternal moral law; and he must, in conformity with this law, give eternity to all rational beings, to whom this law applies and from whom it demands eternity. There must therefore be an *eternal God*, and every moral being must endure eternally, if the final purpose of the moral law is not to be impossible.[16]

We call these propositions *postulates* of reason, since they are immediately connected with, and inseparable from, the requirement

---

[16] The following passage (as far as note 17 below) was introduced in the second edition, replacing this sentence in the first edition: 'These are the postulates of reason which for the sake of our moral determination by them we must accept, not as objectively certain but as subjectively valid for our – that is, human – way of thinking.'

of reason to give to us finite beings a practical *law*. That is, these propositions are not *commanded* by the law, which a *practical* law cannot do for *theorems*, but rather they must necessarily be assumed if reason is to be legislative. Now such an assumption, which the possibility of acknowledging a law in general obliges us to make, we call *a belief*.

However, these propositions are based merely on the application of the moral law to *finite* beings (as has been sufficiently demonstrated above from its deduction) but not on the possibility of the law in itself, the investigation of which is transcendent for us; therefore, in this form they are only *subjective*, i.e., only for finite natures. But since they are based on the mere concept of moral finitude, irrespective of any special modifications of it, they are [42] *universally valid* for these finite natures. How the infinite understanding might view its existence and properties, we cannot know without ourselves being the infinite understanding.

The determinations in the concept of God, established by reason as determined practically by the moral commandment, can be divided into two principal classes. The first contains those determinations which the concept of God itself yields immediately, namely, that he be determined wholly and alone by the moral law;* the second contains those which belong to him in relation to the possibility of finite moral beings, which is precisely why we had to assume his existence.[17] The first determinations present God as the most perfect Holiness, in which the moral law is presented as fully observed, as the ideal of all moral perfection; and simultaneously they present him as the Only Blessed One because he is the Only Holy One, hence as the presentation of the achieved final purpose of practical reason, as the *highest good* itself, whose possibility it postulated. The second determinations present him as the supreme World Sovereign according to moral laws, as Judge of all rational spirits. The first determinations regard him in and for himself, according to his *being*; and he appears through them as the most perfect observer of the moral law. The second determinations regard him according to the effects of this being on other moral beings; and he is by virtue of them the highest executor of the promises of

---

* When one speaks of God, the claim of practical reason on him is not called commandment but law. It declares of him no 'ought,' but rather an 'is'; in regard to him it is not *imperative* but *constitutive*.

[17] See note 16 above.

the moral law, subordinated to no one, hence also the lawgiver – a consequence, however, which is not yet immediately clear but is to be discussed more extensively below. Now as long as we stay with these truths as such we have, to be sure, a *theology*, which we needed in order not to set our theoretical convictions and our practical determination of the will in contradiction; but we still have no *religion*, which would itself in turn have an influence on this [43] determination of the will as cause. How then does religion arise out of theology?

Theology is mere science, dead information without practical influence; religion, however, according to the meaning of the word (*religio*), is supposed to be something that *binds* us – and binds even *more strongly* than we were without it. How far this meaning of the word is strictly applicable here must follow forthwith.

Now it appears at first that theology, based on such principles, could never be mere science without practical influence; but rather that it, being caused by a previous determination of the faculty of desire, must in return have a counter-effect on it. With every determination of the lower faculty of desire, we must assume at least the possibility of the object of our desire; and only by this assumption does the desire, which was previously blind and irrational, become justified and theoretically rational. So here this counter-effect takes place immediately. The determination of the higher faculty of desire to will the good, however, is rational *in itself*, for it occurs immediately by a law of reason and needs no justification through acknowledging the possibility of its object. Not to acknowledge this possibility, however, would be contrary to reason, and hence here the relationship is reversed. In the case of the lower faculty of desire, determination first occurs through the object; in the case of the higher, the object is first realized through determination of the will.

The concept of something that is simply *right*,* is present a priori

---

* The word *right* (which is to be distinguished from *a right*, of which the teachers of natural right speak) has an emphasis peculiar to itself, because it is not capable of a comparative degree. Nothing is *so good*, or *so noble*, that something still *better* or *nobler* could not be conceived; but *right* is only one: everything to which this concept is applicable is either simply right or simply wrong, and there is no third possibility. Neither the Latin *honestum* nor the Greek καλον κἀγαθον has this emphasis. (Perhaps the Latin *par – egisti uti par est* – ?) It is fortunate for our language [44]

in our nature, independent of natural concepts and the experience possible through them. Here we refer in particular to the concept of the necessary congruency of the degree of happiness of a [44] rational being, or one regarded as such, with the degree of his moral perfection. If we regard this idea merely as a concept, without regard to the faculty of desire determined by it, it can be and become for us nothing more than a law given to our judgment by reason for the purpose of reflecting on certain things in nature in order to regard them in another respect than that of their *being*, namely, in that of how they *ought to be*. In this case it appears at first that we would remain completely indifferent to the agreement with this idea and feel neither satisfaction nor interest in it.

But even then, everything external to us that was found to agree with the concept of right which is present in us a priori, would be purposive for a manner of reflecting upon things which is imposed on us by reason; and since all purposiveness is viewed with satisfaction, it would have to excite a feeling of pleasure in us. And indeed, so it is in reality. Joy is universal over the failure of evil purposes and over the discovery and punishment of the villain, just as over the success of honest endeavors, over the recognition of misunderstood virtue, and over the compensation of the righteous for the insults suffered and the sacrifices made along the way of virtue. This joy is grounded in the innermost core of human nature and is the inexhaustible source of the interest we take in works of literature. We find satisfaction in such a world, where everything is in accord with the rule of right, far more than in the real world, where we think we discover such manifold offenses against it. [45]

Something can also please us, however, without our feeling interest in it, i.e., without our desiring the existence of the object. Satisfaction in the beautiful, for example, is of this kind. If the situation were the same in the case of satisfaction in the right, it would be an object of our mere approval. If ever an object were given to us that corresponded to this concept, we could not avoid feeling pleasure; and at the sight of an object that contradicted it, displeasure. But still no desire would thereby arise in us that something to which this concept is applicable might be given in general.

---

that this word has not been robbed of its emphasis through misuse of it. No doubt it owes this good fortune to the taste for the superlative, and for exaggeration – for example, to the notion that not very much is said when one calls an action *right*, and that it must at least be termed *noble*.

So here there would be merely a determination of the feeling of pleasure and displeasure, without the slightest determination of the faculty of desire.

Setting aside the fact that the concept of *ought* already indicates a determination of the faculty of desire to will the existence of a certain object, it is just as universally confirmed by experience that we apply this concept to certain objects necessarily and demand their agreement with it unremittingly. So in the world of literature, in tragedies or novels, we are not satisfied until at least the honor of the innocent victim is rescued and his innocence recognized, and the unjust persecutor is unmasked and has suffered just punishment – however in keeping it may be with the usual course of things in the world that this not happen. This is sure proof that we cannot bring ourselves to regard objects such as the actions of moral beings and their consequences merely according to the causality of natural laws, but rather that we must necessarily compare them with the concept of right. We say in such cases, The play is not finished. And likewise with events in the real world – when we see, for example, the villain in highest prosperity crowned with honor and good, or see the virtuous misunderstood, persecuted, and dying under a thousand torments – here, too, we cannot be satisfied if everything is now supposed to be over and the theater closed for ever. Our [46] satisfaction with what is right, therefore, is no mere approval but is combined with interest.

But there can indeed by a satisfaction combined with interest without our therefore ascribing to this satisfaction a causality for producing its object – without our wanting, or even being able to want, to contribute even just minutely to the existence of its object. In that case the desire for this existence is an *idle wish (pium desiderium)*. We may desire it as fervently as we will, but we must still resign ourselves to the fact that we can make no rightly grounded claim to it. The desire for many kinds of pleasure is thus an idle wish. Who does not desire, for example, a fair day after incessant stormy weather? But we can ascribe to such a desire no causality at all for producing such a day.

If the case of satisfaction in the morally good were like that of any of the things we have cited, we could have no theology and would need no religion. For in that case, however ardently we might wish for the endurance of moral beings and for an almighty, omniscient, and just requiter of their actions, it would still be very presumptuous to infer from a mere wish, however universal and intense it be, the reality of its object, and to accept it even as only subjectively valid.

However, the determination of the faculty of desire by the moral law to will the right ought to have a causality for actually producing it, at least in part. We are immediately obliged to regard the right in our own nature as dependent on ourselves; and when we discover something in ourselves that is contrary to its concept, we feel not mere displeasure, as when an idle wish is unfulfilled, or even just annoyance with ourselves, as in the absence of an object of our interest through our own fault (as in neglecting a rule of [47] discretion), but rather we feel remorse, shame, self-contempt. As far as the right *in us* is concerned, therefore, the moral law in us absolutely requires a causality for producing it; but as far as the right *outside us* is concerned, it cannot directly require such a causality because we cannot regard it as immediately dependent on ourselves, since the latter must be produced not by moral laws but by physical force. So as far as the latter is concerned, the moral law effects in us a mere desire for the right but no attempt to produce it. This desire for the right outside ourselves, i.e., for a Happiness appropriate to the degree of our morality, has actually arisen *through the moral law*. To desire Happiness in general is, to be sure, a natural impulse; in accordance with this impulse, however, we desire it unconditionally, without limitation, and without the slightest regard for anything outside ourselves. But with moral concepts, i.e., as rational beings, we soon resign ourselves to being able only to desire just that measure of Happiness of which we are worthy; and this limitation of the impulse to Happiness is deeply imprinted, even in the most uneducated men, independent of all religious teaching. It is the ground of all judgment about the purposiveness of human fortunes, and it is that prejudice which is most widespread among precisely the least educated portion of mankind, which holds that he must be an especially evil person who encounters especially dismal fortunes.

But this desire is neither *idle* – i.e., one whose satisfaction we would certainly be glad to see, but whose nonsatisfaction would likewise leave us in peace – nor is it unjustified. Rather, the moral law makes *the right in us* into the condition for *the right outside us*. (This does not mean that the law requires obedience from us only under the condition that we may expect Happiness appropriate to it, for the law commands without any conditions, but rather that it presents all Happiness as possible for us only as a condition of our obedience; that is to say, the command is what is unconditioned, but the Happiness is what is conditioned by it.) And the moral [48] law does this by commanding our actions to submit to the principle of universal validity, since the *universal effectiveness* (not merely validity) *of the moral law* and the *Happiness fully appropriate to the degree of morality of every rational being* are identical concepts. Now if the rule of right never would nor could come to be universally effective, that requirement of the causality of the moral law to produce the right in us would thus remain always there as a fact, but it would simply be impossible for it to be fulfilled *in concreto* in a nature like ours. For just as soon as we asked ourselves in the case of a moral action, But what am I doing? our theoretical reason would have to answer us, I am struggling to make possible something that is simply impossible, I am chasing after a chimera, I am obviously acting irrationally. And as soon as we listened again to the voice of the law, we would have to conclude: I am obviously thinking irrationally by declaring that to be impossible which is established for me absolutely as the principle of all my actions. Consequently, however persistent may be the requirement of the moral law that it have a causality in us, a continuous fulfillment of it according to rules would be simply impossible under these circumstances. Our disobedience or obedience would depend, rather, on whether the utterance of the theoretical or that of the practical reason predominated in our mind (whereby in the latter case, however, obviously the possibility of the final purpose of the moral law, denied theoretically, would be silently assumed and acknowledged by our action), about which we would be unable to determine anything according to the cancelled power of the practical faculty over the theoretical; consequently, we would be neither free beings, nor moral, nor capable of imputation, but rather once again a game of chance or a machine determined by natural laws. Regarded *in concreto*, therefore, theology constructed on these principles is never mere science but rather becomes religion immediately in its inception inasmuch as it alone makes possible a continuous causality [49] of the moral law in us by cancelling the contradiction between our theoretical and our practical reason.

And this also shows, as we remind ourselves only in passing, the real force of the moral proof for the existence of God. People had always believed that it was easy to see how from theoretically acknowledged truths one can derive consequences that have precisely the degree of certainty as the truths on which they are based – how, for example, from our dependence on God, theoretically demonstrated a priori, there will follow the duty to conduct oneself towards him in accordance with this dependence. They believed it was easy because they had accustomed themselves to this procedure of making inferences, although it is really not comprehensible at all because it is not correct, since no power over practical reason can be ascribed to the theoretical reason. On the other hand, however, theoretical propositions can be derived from a practical commandment which is absolutely a priori and is not based on any theoretical propositions as its premises, because to the practical reason a power certainly is to be ascribed over the theoretical, though suitable to its own laws. It is thus quite the opposite procedure for making inferences; and if it has been misunderstood, this is merely because the moral law has not been thought of as utterly a priori, and its causality as utterly necessary (not theoretically, but practically).

The contradiction between theoretical and practical reason is now removed, and the administration of right has been transferred to a being in whom the rule of right is not merely *universally valid* but is *universally effective* – that is, to a being who can also assure us the right outside ourselves.

The rule is universally effective for nature, which is not moral but does have influence on the Happiness of moral beings. Insofar as the conduct of other moral beings enters into this Happiness, they too can be regarded as nature. In this respect God is the determiner of the effects produced in nature by the causality of their will, [50] but not of their will itself.

Moral beings, however, *as such* – i.e., in respect of their will – cannot be determined like amoral nature by the will of the universal lawgiver, lest they cease to be moral; and the determination of the former by this will must be something completely different from that of the latter, if their possibility is to show itself. The latter [nature] can never itself become moral but can only be set in agreement with the moral ideas of a rational being; the former [moral beings] should be free, and should be first causes of moral determinations solely by themselves. As far as the latter is concerned, therefore, God is not actually lawgiver, but rather mover, determiner; it is the mere instrument, and the only one who acts morally is he.

Moral beings, however, are parts of nature, not only insofar as they are *active* according to natural laws, but also insofar as they are *passive* according to the same laws. As such they are the object of the determination of nature according to moral ideas, insofar as the proper degree of Happiness is allotted to them by these ideas; and as such they are fully within the moral order, whenever the degree of their Happiness is fully appropriate to the degree of their moral perfection.

Now by this means we first come, if I may so express myself, into correspondence with God. We are obliged in all our decisions to look to him as the only one who knows precisely their moral worth, since he has to determine our fortunes according to them, and whose approval or disapproval is the only proper judgment of them. Our fear, our hope, all our expectations are in relation to him; only in his concept of us do we find our true worth. The holy reverence for God, which must thereby arise in us necessarily, combined with the desire for the Happiness to be expected only from him, does not determine our higher faculty of desire to will the right in general (this it can never do, since it is itself based on the already completed determination of the higher faculty of desire); it determines, rather, our empirically determinable will actually [51] to produce the right in ourselves persistently and continuously. This is already religion, therefore, based on the idea of God as the determiner of nature according to moral purposes and, in us, on the desire for Happiness – which, however, increases and strengthens not our obligation to virtue but only our desire to satisfy this obligation.

However, the universal effectiveness of the divine will for us as *passive* beings allows us further to infer its universal validity for us also as active beings. God directs us according to a law that can be given to him in no other way than by *his* reason – consequently, according to his will as determined by the moral law. Thus his judgment is based on his *will as universally effective law* for rational beings, even insofar as they are active, since their agreement with his will is the standard according to which their portion of Happiness is allotted to them as passive beings. The applicability of this standard becomes clear at once from the fact that reason can never contradict itself but must give precisely the same testimony in all rational beings; hence, the will of God determined by the moral law must be fully identical with the law given to us by the very same reason. It is accordingly a matter of complete indifference for the *legality* of our actions whether we arrange them in accordance with the rational law because our reason commands, or because God wills what our reason requires – whether we derive our obligation from the command of reason alone or from the will of God. Whether it is a matter of complete indifference for the *morality* of our actions, however, is not yet clear from this and needs further investigation.

To derive our obligation from the will of God means to acknowledge his will *as such* to be our law, to consider oneself obligated to holiness because he requires it of us. So we are speaking, then, not merely of an accomplishment of the will of God according to the matter of volition, but rather of an obligation based on its [52] form: we act in accordance with the law of reason because it is *God's* law.

Here arise the following two questions: Is there an obligation to obey the will of God as such, and on what could it be based? And then: How do we recognize the law of reason in us as the law of God? We proceed to the answer of the first.

The concept of God is already given to us by our reason alone, and is realized by it alone, insofar as it commands a priori; and there is simply no other conceivable way in which we could arrive at this concept. Furthermore, reason obligates us to obey its law without referring back to a lawgiver above itself, so that it confuses itself and is simply destroyed and ceases to be reason if one assumes that there is still something other than itself which commands it. Now if reason presents the will of God to us as completely identical with its own law, it certainly obligates us indirectly to obey it also; but this obligation is based on nothing but its agreement with its own law, and no obedience to God is possible except out of obedience to reason. Now from this it is clear in the first place that it does not matter at all even for the *morality* of our actions whether we consider ourselves obligated to something because our reason commands it or because God commands it. But from this, one cannot yet see at all what purpose the latter representation is supposed to serve, since its efficacy already presupposes the efficacy of the former, since the mind must already be determined to want to obey reason before the will to obey God is possible – since it appears, therefore, that the latter representation could determine us neither more universally nor more strongly than the one on which it depends and through which it first becomes possible. But granted that it could be shown that under certain conditions it really does broaden the determination of our will, yet it must still be decided in advance whether there occurs an obligation to make use of it in general. [53] And it follows, then, directly from the above that although reason obligates us to obey the will of God according to its content (*voluntati ejus materialiter spectatae*) because this is completely identical with the law of reason, yet it directly requires no obedience except to its own law, on no other ground than because it is its law. Consequently, since only direct practical laws of reason are obligatory, it does not obligate us to any obedience to the will of God as such (*voluntatem ejus formaliter spectatam*). Hence practical reason contains no command to think of the will of God, as such, as legislative for us, but contains merely a permission; and should we find a posteriori that this representation determines us more strongly, then wisdom can advise us to make use of it, but the use of this representation can never be a duty. There occurs, therefore, no obligation to religion, i.e., to the acknowledgment of God as moral lawgiver. All the less so, since however necessary it is to assume the existence of God and the immortality of our soul – because without this assumption the required causality of the moral law in us is not possible at all, and this necessity is just as universally valid as the moral law itself – still we cannot even say that we are *obligated* to assume these propositions, because obligation applies only to the practical. The extent to which the representation of God as lawgiver through this law in us is valid, however, depends on the extension of its influence on the determination of the will, and this in turn depends on the conditions under which rational beings can be determined by it. If it could be shown, namely, that this representation were necessary in order to give the force of law to the command of reason in general (though in fact the opposite has been shown), it would then be valid for all rational beings. If it can be shown that it facilitates the determination of the will in all *finite* rational beings, then it is generally valid for them. If the conditions under which it facilitates and broadens this determination are [54] conceivable only for human nature, then it is valid for all human beings, supposing that they are situated in universal properties of human nature; or, if they are situated in its particular properties, it is valid only for some human beings.

The determination of the will to obey the law of God in general can take place only through the law of practical reason and is to be presupposed as a lasting and permanent decision of the mind. However, particular cases of the application of the law can be conceived in which reason alone would not have sufficient power to determine the will but in order to strengthen its efficacy would also need the representation that a certain action is commanded by God. This insufficiency of the rational command as such can have no other ground than a lessening of our respect for reason in this particular case. And this respect can have been lessened only by a conflicting natural law, which determines our inclination, and which appears together with the law of reason that determines our higher faculty of desire *in one and the same subject*, namely, *in us*. Hence, if the dignity of the law is determined solely according to that of the legislative subject, this natural law could appear to be of the same rank and worth as the law of reason. Here we may abstract completely from the fact that we could deceive ourselves in such a case, that we might not hear the voice of duty for the screaming of inclination but could fancy ourselves in the position where we stand under natural laws alone. Rather, we may presuppose that we correctly distinguish the requirements of the two laws and their boundaries, and that we recognize undeniably what our duty is in this case. Nevertheless, it can easily happen that we decide just this once to make an exception to the universal rule, just this once to act contrary to the clear declaration of reason, because we believe that in doing so we are responsible to no one but ourselves, and because we think it is our business whether we wish to act rationally or irrationally. It would matter to no one but ourselves if we subject ourselves to the disadvantage that must certainly result from [55] this if there is a moral judge of our actions, through which punishment our disobedience seems as it were to be expiated; we would be sinning at our own risk. Such a lack of respect for reason is thus based on lack of respect for ourselves, for which we believe we can take responsibility on our own. But if the duty that occurs in this case appears to us as commanded by God, or if the law of reason appears thoroughly and in all its applications as God's law, which amounts to the same thing, then it appears in a being regarding whom it is not a matter of our discretion whether we will respect him or refuse him proper respect. By every conscious disobedience to this being, we make not simply an exception to the rule, but we directly deny reason in general. We are sinning not merely against a rule derived from reason but against its first commandment. Apart from responsibility for the punishment that we could in any case take upon ourselves, we are now responsible to a being, the mere thought of whom must impress upon us the deepest reverence, and whom not to honor is the highest foolishness – and responsible, too, for refusing the reverence due to him, which is not to be expiated by any punishment.

The idea of God, as lawgiver through the moral law in us, is thus based on an alienation of what is ours, on translating something subjective into a being outside us; and this alienation is the real *principle of religion*, insofar as it is to be used for determining the will. In the truest sense it cannot strengthen our respect for the moral law in general, because all respect for God is based solely on his acknowledged agreement with this law, and hence on respect for the law itself. But it can increase our respect for its decisions in particular cases, where a strong counterweight of inclination emerges. And so it is clear how, even though reason must first determine us in general to obey the will of God, in particular cases the representation of this will may nevertheless determine us in [56] return to obey reason.

Yet it is to be remembered in passing that this respect for God and the respect for the moral law as his law, which is based upon it, must be based solely on its agreement with this law – i.e., on his holiness – because only under this condition is it respect for the moral law, which must alone be the incentive for every purely moral action. If it were based, let us say, on the desire to ingratiate oneself into his goodness or on fear of his justice, our obedience would not be based on respect for God at all but rather on selfishness.

Inclinations conflicting with duty are surely to be assumed in all finite beings, for the concept of the finite in morality is precisely the fact that it is determined by yet other laws than the moral law, i.e., by the laws of its nature. And no ground can be given to explain why natural laws should under any condition always and ever harmonize with the moral law for natural beings, on whatever exalted level they may stand. But it can by no means be determined why and in what way this conflict of inclination with law should necessarily so weaken respect for the latter as merely rational law that in order to operate actively it must in addition be hallowed by the idea of a divine legislation. And we cannot restrain ourselves from feeling a far greater admiration for every rational being who does not need this representation to determine his will – not because inclination is weaker in him, in which case it would have no merit, but because respect for reason is stronger in him – than we feel for one who does need it. Religion, therefore, insofar as it is not mere belief in the postulates of practical reason but is to be used as a factor in determining the will, cannot even be assured of subjective universal validity for human beings (for only this kind can be under discussion here) – although, on the other hand, we also cannot [57] prove that a virtue is possible for finite beings in general, or for human beings in this earthly life in particular, which is able to dispense with this factor entirely.

Now this transfer of legislative authority to God is based, in consequence of the above, on the fact that a law must be given to him by his own reason, which is valid for us because he directs us according to it, and which must be completely identical with that given to us by our own reason, according to which we are supposed to act. Here, then, two laws, which in themselves are completely independent of each other, come together merely in their principle, pure practical reason, both conceived to be valid *for us*, completely identical in respect of their content, and different merely in respect of the subjects in whom they are found. We can now conclude for certain in every requirement of the moral law in us that an identical requirement is issued to us in God, that the commandment of the law in us is therefore God's commandment, too, according to *matter*. However, we still cannot say that the commandment of the law in us is God's commandment *as such*, hence according to *form*. In order to be able to assume the latter, we would have to have a ground for regarding the moral law in us as dependent on the moral law in God for us – i.e., for assuming the will of God as its cause.

Now it seems to be quite immaterial whether we view the commands of our reason as completely identical with God's command to us, or whether we view them as themselves the commands of God directly. In part, however, the concept of legislation is fully completed only by the latter; but in part, and above all, in the conflict of inclination and duty the latter representation must necessarily add a new gravity to the commandment of reason.

Assuming the will of God as cause of the moral law in us can mean two things: namely, that God's will is either the cause of the *content* of the moral law, or that it is only the cause of *the existence of the moral law in us*. It is already clear from the above that [58] the former is simply not to be assumed, for heteronomy of reason would thereby be introduced, and right would be subjected to an unconditioned arbitrariness, which means that there would be no right at all. Whether the latter is conceivable and whether a rational ground for it can be found needs further investigation.

The question, therefore, with whose answer we are now concerned, is this: Do we find any ground for viewing God as the cause for the existence of the moral law in us? Or, expressed as a problem: We have to seek a principle from which God's will would be recognized as the ground of the existence of the moral law in us. It is clear from the above that the moral law in us contains God's law to us and is *materialiter* his law. Whether it is his law also according to form – i.e., promulgated by him and as his own, as that by which the concept of legislation is made complete – that is now the question, which therefore can also be expressed thus: Has God really promulgated his law to us? Can we demonstrate a fact that confirms itself as such a promulgation?

If this question were raised for theoretical purposes, merely in order to extend our knowledge, we could satisfy ourselves without even answering it and could be certain a priori (before its answer) that an answer satisfactory for this purpose is not possible at all, since it is asking for the cause of something supernatural, namely, the moral law in us, and the category of causality is therefore being applied to a noumenon. But since it is asked for practical purposes in order to extend the determination of the will, in the first place we cannot reject it so flatly, and in the second place we resign ourselves from the start to be satisfied even with an answer that is valid only subjectively, i.e., for our laws of thought.

Division of Religion in General
Into Natural and Revealed[18]

Theology becomes religion, in its *most universal* meaning, whenever the propositions assumed by the law of reason for determining our will operate upon us practically. This effect *may* take place [1] in our entire faculty, in order to produce a harmony in its different functions by setting theoretical and practical reason in agreement and making possible in us the postulated causality of the latter. In this way unity is first brought about in the person, and all functions of his faculty are guided towards a single final purpose. *Or* [2], this effect may take place particularly – this is, negatively – in our faculty of sensation by effecting profound reverence for the highest ideal of all perfection, and trust, holy awe, and thankfulness for the only true judge of our morality and just determiner of our fortunes according to it. These sensations are not actually supposed to determine the will; but they are supposed to increase the efficacy of the determination that has already taken place. One would do well, however, not to work towards an unlimited heightening of these sensations, especially insofar as they are based on the concept of God as our moral judge (and which together constitute what is termed *piety*), because injury could thereby occur to the proper impetus of all morality: willing what is right simply *because* it is right. *Or* [3], finally, this effect may take place immediately in our will by the impetus, added to the gravity of the commandment, that it is God's commandment; and thereby arises religion in its *most proper* meaning.

It is already clear from the concept of God as independent executor of the rational law in general that the moral law in us is to be accepted as God's law in us according to its content. Whether we have grounds for assuming it as such also according to its [60] form is the question to be investigated now. Since in this case it is not a matter of the law in itself, as we have it in ourselves, but rather of the author of the law, we are able here in the concept of

[18] *Gesamtausgabe*, pp. 36–41 (§3).

divine legislation to abstract completely from its content (*materia*) and have only to look at its form. The present task, therefore, is this: to search for a principle from which God would be recognized as moral lawgiver. Or, the question is, Has God proclaimed himself to us as moral lawgiver, and *how* has he done it?

This can be conceived as possible in two ways: namely, that it has taken place either *in us* as moral beings, in our rational nature, or *outside it*. Now there is nothing in our reason, insofar as it is legislative purely a priori, that would justify our assuming this. We must therefore look around for something outside our reason that refers us back to it again so as to be able to infer more from its laws than they alone entitle us; or else we must give up entirely the attempt to recognize God as lawgiver from this principle. Outside our rational nature is that which is present to us for observation and knowledge, the world of sense. Everywhere in this world we find order and purposiveness; everything leads us to its origin according to concepts of a rational being. But for all the purposes to which we are led by observing it, our reason must seek an ultimate, a final purpose, as the unconditioned to the conditioned. However, everything in our knowledge is conditioned except for the purpose of the highest good, established in us by practical reason, which is commanded absolutely and unconditionally. This alone, therefore, is capable of being the final purpose we seek; and we are urged by the subjective character of our nature to acknowledge it as such. No being was able to have this final purpose except the one whose practical faculty is determined solely by the moral law; and none was able to adapt nature to this law except the one who determines natural laws by himself. This being is God. God is therefore *creator of the world*. No being is capable of being the object of this [61] final purpose except moral beings, because they alone are capable of the highest good. We ourselves, therefore, as moral beings, are (objectively) the final purpose of creation. But we are also, as sensuous beings – i.e., as beings who stand under natural laws – parts of creation; and the entire arrangement of our nature, insofar as it depends on these laws, is the work of the creator – i.e., of the determiner of natural laws by his moral nature. Now in part, it obviously does not depend on nature that reason speaks this way in us and not otherwise; in part, it would be thoroughly dialectical to ask whether it depends on nature that *we* are moral beings. For, in the first place, we would then conceive the concept of morality to be absent from ourselves and would nevertheless assume that we would still be *ourselves* in that case – i.e., that we would have retained our identity – which cannot be assumed. In the second place, the question aims at objective assertions in the field of the supersensuous, in which we may assert nothing objectively.* But it does not matter *to us* at all whether we are not *conscious* of the commandment of the moral law in ourselves, or whether we are not moral beings at all; furthermore, our self-consciousness stands completely under natural laws. Therefore, it follows quite correctly that it is due to the arrangement of the sensuous nature of finite beings that they *are conscious* of the moral law in themselves – and we may add, if only we have previously determined ourselves correctly, that they *are* moral beings. Since, then, God is the author of this arrangement, the proclamation of the moral law in us through self-consciousness is to be regarded as his proclamation, and the final purpose which self-consciousness establishes for us, as his final purpose which he had in producing us. Just as we recognize him to be the creator of our nature, so we must acknowledge him also to be our moral [62] lawgiver, because only through just such an arrangement was consciousness of the moral law in ourselves possible for us. This proclamation of God himself takes place, then, through the supernatural in us; and we must not be misled by the fact that in order to recognize it we had to make use of a concept outside it, namely, that of nature. For in part it was reason that delivered to us that without which this concept could not have served our purposes at all, the concept of the possible final purpose, and thereby made possible for the first time the knowledge of God as creator. And in part, even this knowledge could still not have presented God to us as lawgiver without the moral law in us, the existence of which is just the proclamation of God that we are seeking.

The second way that we were able to conceive of how God could proclaim himself as moral lawgiver was *outside* of the supernatural in us, thus in the *world of sense*, since besides these two we have no third object. We can infer something supernatural, however, neither from the concept of the world in general nor from any object or occurrence within it in particular, by means of natural concepts,

* The question, Why should there be moral beings at all? is easy to answer: because of the requirement of the moral law on God to further the highest good outside himself, which is possible only through the existence of rational beings.

which are the only ones applicable to the sensuous world. But something supernatural is the basis of the concept of a proclamation of God as moral lawgiver. Consequently, this would have to happen through a fact in the world of sense, whose causality we would posit *forthwith*, hence without first inferring, in a supernatural being, and whose purpose – to be a proclamation of God as moral lawgiver – we would recognize *at once*, i.e., directly by perception. So it must happen if this case is to be possible at all.

Now to begin with, this investigation presents two principles of religion, insofar as it is based on acknowledgment of a formal legislation of God. The one is the principle of the supernatural *in us*; the other is the principle of a supernatural *outside us*. The possibility of the first has already been shown; the possibility of the second, which is really the matter at hand, we must set forth further. A religion based upon the first principle we can call natural [63] religion, since it makes use of the concept of a nature in general. And one based on the second, since it is supposed to reach us through a mysterious, supernatural means that is determined quite precisely for this end, we call *revealed religion*. Subjectively regarded, as *habitus* of a rational spirit (as religiousness), both religions can indeed be united in one individual and constitute a single religion, since they have opposed but not contradictory principles.

Before we proceed, we need still to note that since merely a principle of legislation according to its form has been under discussion here, while we have abstracted completely from its content, we could not be concerned with investigating the proper place for the legislation according to its content (*legislatio materialiter spectata*) in consequence of these two different principles. It is self-evidently clear right away that according to the first principle, which posits in us the proclamation of the lawgiver, even the legislation itself is to be sought in us – namely, in our rational nature. According to the second principle, however, two cases are once again possible: either the proclamation of the lawgiver outside us refers us back to our rational nature, and the entire revelation, expressed in words, says only that God is lawgiver, that the law written in your hearts is his law; or, it goes on to prescribe his law especially for us, in just the way in which it makes God known as lawgiver. In a revelation given *in concreto*, nothing prevents both from being able to occur.

Since the appearance of the critical philosophy, the question has already been raised more than once, How is revealed religion possible? – a question that always obtruded itself but could be properly posed only since this light illumined the path of our investigations. But it seems to me that in all the attempts, at least that I know, the knot has more often been [64] cut than untied. One attempt correctly deduces the possibility of religion in general, develops its content, establishes its criteria; and then by three colossal leaps – (1) by confusing the broadest meaning of religion with the narrowest, (2) by confusing natural and revealed religion, (3) by confusing revealed in general with Christian – arrives at the proposition: the Christian religion is fully such a rational religion. Another attempt, from whom it indeed could not be concealed that the former religion is still something more, places this 'more' merely in the greater sensuous objectification of the abstract ideas of the latter. But reason a priori gives no law at all, and is able to give none, concerning the way in which we should represent to ourselves the ideas realized through its postulates. Everyone, even the sharpest thinker, I believe, thinks of them with some admixture of sensibility whenever he applies them to himself for practical purposes; and so it proceeds in imperceptible steps, right down to the most crudely sensuous human being. No religion is completely pure from sensibility *in concreto*; for religion in general is based on the need of sensibility. But the greater or lesser degree does not justify any classification. Then where do the limits of rational religion end according to this manner of representation, and where do those of revealed religion begin? There would be as many religions, according to it, as there were written or oral teachings about religious truths – as many as there were subjects in general who believed in a religion. Why precisely this or that presentation of religious truths should be the most authorized one can be made comprehensible by nothing but its origin; and where the appeal to a supernatural authority may come from, which we find as the characteristic mark of all alleged revelations, can be made comprehensible by nothing at all. This aberration from the only possible way of deducing the concept of revelation came about merely from neglecting that universally known rule of logic: concepts that are supposed to justify a classification must be included under a higher generic concept but must be specifically different among themselves. The concept of religion in general is a generic concept. If natural and revealed religion, as included under it, are to be [65] specifically different, they must be so as regards their content; or if this is not possible, as can already be surmised a priori, they must be so at least as regards their principles of cognition. Otherwise, the entire classification is empty, and we must completely relinquish the warrant for assuming a revealed religion. For the concept indicated above is also the one that linguistic usage has connected with the word *revelation* from time immemorial. All the founders of religions have appealed for proof of the truth of their doctrines not to the determination of our reason, nor to theoretical proofs, but rather to a supernatural authority, and have required belief in this as the only legitimate way to conviction.[19]

[19] In the first edition the text continues as follows: 'They have not given the appearance of developing something that was already present in us but

rather of telling us something wholly new, unknown. They have not wished to pass for wise, philanthropic leaders, but for inspired emissaries of the Deity – by what right, we will only be able to answer below; or rather, it will answer itself.' I. H. Fichte retains this passage in footnote form in the *Sämmtliche Werke* as a 'supplement from the first edition.'

§5

Formal Discussion of the Concept of Revelation
In Preparation for a Material
Discussion of It[20]

Beginning with the concept of religion, we arrived in the previous chapter at the concept of a possible revelation that might have religious principles for its material. If that possibility of the concept, now merely presupposed, should be confirmed, it would be the *material locus* of this concept in our understanding. We shall now locate it also according to its *form*, not for the sake of systematic necessity, but to promote clarity.

Revelation, according to form, is a kind of *making known*; and everything that holds good for this genus also holds good for it.

There are two *internal* conditions of all making known: namely, something that is made known, the *material*; and then the [66] way in which it is made known, the *form* of the making known. There are likewise two *external* conditions: one who makes known, and one to whom it is made known. We proceed from the internal conditions.

What is made known becomes something *made* known only by my not already knowing it beforehand. If I knew it already, the other person makes known to me only the fact that he knew it, too; and in that case the material of the making known is something else. Things that everyone of necessity knows cannot be made known. Knowledge that is possible a priori, or philosophical knowledge, is developed; the other person is led to it. I *demonstrate* to someone a mistake in his reasoning or the equality of two triangles, but I do not *make* them *known* to him. Knowledge that is possible only a posteriori, historical knowledge, is made known – but not *proved*, because one finally hits upon something that is not to be derived a priori, the testimony of empirical sensibility. Such knowledge is taken on authority. Authority is trust in our power of correct observation and in our veracity.

Of course, knowledge possible a priori can also be taken on authority, as the artisan, for example, accepts so many mathematical

20 This chapter was added in the second edition. *Gesamtausgabe*, pp. 153–61.

propositions without investigation and proof, on the testimony of others and of his own experience of their applicability. Now such a knowledge is in itself, according to its material, philosophical; but according to its form in the subject, merely historical. His acceptance is based ultimately on the testimony of the inner sense of the one who has investigated the proposition and deemed it true.

First corollary. Only knowledge that is historical, at least according to form, or also according to matter – thus, only perceptions – can be made known. If further inferences are built (*comparative*) on such perceptions, if universal truths are derived from them, then from here on nothing more is *made known*, but only *demonstrated*.

If perceptions, to proceed to the second internal characteristic [67] of making known, can be made known only in the form of historical knowledge, they are themselves to that extent not form but material; they must consequently be given to receptivity. But in that case, except for the external condition of one who makes known, our entire empirical knowledge would be made known, for it is thoroughly given. But if someone occasions a sensation in us directly, we do not say of the resultant knowledge that he makes it known to us, but rather we know it then ourselves. If someone gives us a rose to smell, for example, we do not say that he makes known to us the smell of the rose; that is, he makes known to *us* neither that the rose smells pleasant in general nor to what degree: that can be judged only by direct sensation. However, we surely can say that he has made known to *us how* the rose smells; that is, in our representation he has combined our subject with the representation of a certain experiment. Making known, in the proper sense, takes place only when in our representation not *our* subject but some other subject is connected with the predicate of a perception. Now again, this connection itself certainly occurs in consequence of a subjective perception; but the material of what is made known is not this perception of our subject but another perception of another subject.

Second corollary. The perception that is made known is not direct, but rather it is given through perception of a representation of itself. This perception that is actually made known, then, can extend through a long series of terms; in this case it is transmitted through *tradition*. The supernaturalist, who assumes the existence of God to be knowable only through

revelation, makes this assumption: God says to us that he himself (God) perceives his own existence; now one must surely
trust his (God's) assurance; hence, etc. – which is without [68]
doubt a circular proof.

We now proceed to the external conditions of making known.

Every case of making known includes one who *makes* known.
If we ourselves infer by perceiving another that he must have had a
certain perception, he does not make known to us his perception,
but it discloses itself to us – we discover it ourselves. We therefore
presuppose in one who makes known, a spontaneity with choice,
hence with consciousness; and only in this way does he become one
who makes known.

But he must want to make known to us not just something in
general; he must want to make known to us a certain definite
representation, which he not only has himself, but whose production in us he conceives through the causality of his concept of this
production. Now such a concept is called a concept of purpose.

Third corollary. Every case of making known, therefore, presupposes in the one who makes known a concept of the representation to be produced, as the purpose of his action. Hence,
the one who makes known must be an intelligent being, and
his action must be related to the representation that is thereby
stimulated in the other as *moral ground* to *consequence.*

Making known requires, finally, one to whom something is made
known. If nothing at all is made known to him, or if just what the
other intended is not made known to him, or if it is made known to
him through other means, perhaps, and not through the communication of the other – then at least the making known that was
desired has not occurred.

Fourth corollary. The action of the one who makes known
must consequently be related to the representation produced in
the other as physical cause to effect. That such a relationship is
possible – i.e., that an intelligent being in consequence of a
purposive concept could through freedom become a physical
cause – is postulated for the possibility of a making known in
general, but it cannot be proven theoretically.

The concept of revelation, as included under this generic [69]
concept, must have all of the characteristics indicated, but it may
also have additional ones; i.e., it can fully determine certain
characteristics of making known which are determinable in different

ways. And here, since we are as yet treating this concept merely empirically, we must hold to linguistic usage.

Ordinarily one says *reveal* only in regard to *the matter* of knowledge that is believed to be very important or very deeply hidden – knowledge that not everyone could find. Since this characteristic is merely relative, in that the importance or unimportance, the gravity or lightness of an item of knowledge depends merely on the opinion of the subject, it becomes clear at once that this definition is of no use to philosophy.

Equally useless is another definition in linguistic usage, which is related to *the one who makes known*, namely, where one particularly says 'reveal' only concerning the communication of supramundane beings, daemons. All of the heathen oracles were thus alleged revelations. It is already included in the concept of making known that the one who reveals must be a free and intelligent being, that he must therefore belong to the generic concept to which daemons also belong; but how daemons and men (for example) could be sharply distinguished according to kind, may not follow so easily. All the distinctions would turn out to be only relative.

Accordingly, there would remain for us no precise definition useful for philosophy except this one: that in making known in general, every free spirit is one who makes known, be he finite or infinite, but in revelation it is the Infinite Spirit. This is a meaning which might well be reserved even in ordinary linguistic usage for the words *revelation, reveal,* etc.

The determinations of making known in general hold also for the concept of revelation. Therefore, by means of the third and fourth corollaries, all teachings and knowledge that are possible through contemplation of the sensuous world, whose original ground we must consider to be God, are excluded from the concept of [70] revelation. Nothing is *made* known to us by this contemplation; rather, we ourselves recognize – or rather think we recognize from this – what we ourselves first brought in unnoticed. That is, we contemplate appearances in the world of sense partly as purposes in themselves and partly as means to purposes quite different from that of a possible teaching. Of course, one might believe for a moment that the entire system of appearances could be viewed as revelation, to the extent that a knowledge would *also* be possible by this means *simultaneously*, and in particular a knowledge of God, of our dependence on him, and of our duties resulting from it – to that extent, because this knowledge would be possible, the concept of such a knowledge might be transferred to God and attributed to him as his design in the creation of the world. However, even if we disregard here the fact that such a knowledge of the supersensuous from the sensuous world is completely impossible, and the fact that we brought unnoticed into the sensuous world in the first place the spiritual concepts that are given in a completely different way, which we then believe to have found in it – even so, such a design of God could still not be acknowledged as the *ultimate* one, hence not as the *final purpose* of creation. Knowledge is incapable of being a final purpose; for the question always remains to be answered, Why then am I supposed to know God? Knowledge would be only a means to a higher purpose, and hence not the ultimate design of the creation of the world; and between the latter and the knowledge that is supposed to be its aim, the relationship of ground to consequence would be abolished.

Furthermore, it is by no means necessary even in that system to preserve that knowledge by contemplating the structure of the world. Experience teaches that many people judge it according to quite different laws; hence the relationship of cause to effect is also abolished, and creation is not a revelation.

Revelation, to the extent that we have defined the concept so far, is a perception that is effected in us by God, in accordance with the concept of some teaching to be given by this means (whatever its material may be), as its *purpose*.

This latter relationship, with which we are really concerned [71] here, has also been denoted by the word *immediate*. And this is quite correct, so long as one does not mean thereby to say: our perception is supposed to come *first in the series of efficient causes* after the action of God; it is supposed to be simply B – this is not what matters here at all. (So long as the action of God is simply A, even in this series, then between it and our perception there may be as many intermediate terms as desired.) But it is quite correct, so long as one means thereby to say only this much: God's concept of the teaching to be given is to be A in the series of *final causes*, and our teaching is to be B.

Concerning the logical possibility of this concept, no doubt can arise; for if its determinations were contradictory, this contradiction would soon have been discovered. Its physical possibility is based on the postulate of the moral law that a free, intelligent being may be a cause in the world of sense in conformity with a concept of purpose – which we had to assume for God for the sake of the possibility of a practical law in sensuous beings.

In the application of this concept to a fact, however, great difficulties come into prominence.

Namely, if it were merely a matter of a certain perception and the knowledge thereby intended becoming actual in us without our having had to go back to the ground of the appearance, our investigation would now be finished. We would merely have had to look at the matter of a revelation, which we would simply have had given to us. Least of all are we concerned with the matter, however, but above all with the form of revelation. Not just something in general is supposed to be made known to us, but this 'something' becomes known in particular only by our acknowledging it as revealed. God is supposed to communicate knowledge to us, which becomes knowledge only because the communicator is none other than God.

This comes about because the belief in every case of making known, according to the nature of this concept, can be based on nothing else but the authority of the one who makes known, [72] as was demonstrated above.

The more important question, therefore, which remains to be answered, is this: how are we to know *that* God, in conformity with a concept of purpose, has effected a certain perception in us?

If, for example, someone were to have an appearance that announced itself to him as God and instructed him as such concerning many things, one might perhaps imagine for a moment that this could be the material of the representation produced by the perception. But here the question is precisely how he is supposed to know that this appearance is really effected by God, that neither he himself nor another being is deceiving him. The question is one of causal connection; and these are not *perceived*, but one *infers* them.*

Such an inference might at first appear possible in two ways: namely, either a posteriori, by ascending from the given perception as effect to its cause; or a priori, by descending from the known cause to the effect. We will investigate the possibility of the first inference, which in view of theology people still will not allow to be taken away from them, although everything possible has happened to make its falsity obvious.

* Whoever is indignant that I said this, for him I did not say it. But I know readers to whom one must certainly say it.

There are two ways to ascend from a perception to the knowledge of its cause, which is not perceived as such: namely, either in the series of *efficient* or of *final causes*. In the first case I determine the concept of the cause by the perceived effect. For example, a weight is moved forward. I apply the laws of motion to this perception and infer that the cause is a physical force in space, that it acts with such-and-such force, etc. The perception that is supposed to bring me a posteriori to the concept of revelation must not be explicable according to physical laws; otherwise, I would seek [73] its cause, and find it, in the realm of these laws and would not need to transfer it to the *free* original ground of all laws. The only rational predicate of this cause is therefore *subjective* and *negative*: *it is indeterminable by me* – a predicate to which my unconsciousness of having determined it entitles me fully. In making this subjectively indeterminable *A*, however, into the absolutely and objectively indeterminable *A*, immediately and without any further ground (and none can be given but the unconsciousness of my determining), I am certainly following the propensity of my spirit to advance as quickly as possible to the absolutely unconditioned. But the illegitimacy of this procedure should hardly need any further censure now.

We are certainly obliged to assume in general an absolutely first term in the series; but we may not say for any particular term that *this* is the first. For the series (I am talking about that of *efficient* causes) is infinite, and our ascent in it is never ended. If we end it anywhere, we are assuming an infinite which is finite; and that *is* a contradiction.

What we are unable to do in the series of efficient causes, let us attempt in that of final causes.

We have a perception, and the first thing that follows upon it in time is the perception of knowledge in us which we have not previously perceived in ourselves. We are obliged by the laws of thought to conceive the two perceptions in causal connection: the first is the cause of the second, as its effect. Now conversely we want also to conceive the knowledge as cause of the perception that causes it; i.e., we want to assume that this perception was possible only through the concept of the knowledge that was caused. If we are not driven to this assumption by necessity, then we are assuming something quite arbitrarily and without ground – *we just think so.*
Necessity (whether subjective or objective will be demonstrated

presently) drives us to this assumption only when the [74] perception and the teaching thereby imparted are related as parts to the whole, and when neither a part is conceivable without the whole nor the whole without all of the parts. Such a relationship is not only possible in itself, but it is also actual in many cases of the kind investigated. *I* must then conceive the two things in purposive connection; *I* cannot explain the perception, unless in advance I posit the concept of the knowledge arising thereby – which follows in the *temporal series*, hence in the series of my sensations – in *the series of my judgments*, which are guided by spontaneity. Up to that point I am quite right. Now, however, I transfer the subjective law of the possibility of my judgment to the possibility of the thing in itself and infer that, because I must *conceive* in advance the concept of the effect before the cause, it must therefore also *be* in advance in some intelligent being – an inference to which the propensity to assume everything subjective as objectively valid surely seduces me, but does not justify. No rational conviction can be based on such an obviously surreptitious chain of inferences.

But supposing that we grant you the validity of this inference, you would, to be sure, have grounds for assuming a free, intelligent being as cause of the appearance under investigation, a being for whom the *A* in the series of efficient causes, which for you is indeterminable, would be determinable. And that may be the first, best human being, who knows a little more than you. But what entitles you then to assume it to be precisely the infinite being? What *I* cannot comprehend, only the infinite understanding can comprehend – this inference is presumptuous if ever one was. Far more modest and consistent were the judgments of the heathen theologians who assumed the cause of inexplicable appearances to be simply daemons, certainly not the infinite spirit, and among us the people who explain them as the effects of sorcerers, ghosts, and goblins.

A posteriori, therefore, it is simply impossible theoretically to acknowledge an appearance to be revelation.

Just as impossible is a theoretical proof a priori. One has [75] only to name the requisites of such a proof in order to demonstrate its impossibility and its contradictions. The necessity would have to be demonstrated, namely, from the concept of God given a priori *by theoretical natural philosophy*, that there is present in God the concept of a certain *empirically determined* revelation and the resolve to present it.

We must accordingly give up the possibility of fathoming this concept from the side of its form, and, if no other way should be demonstrated, give up the real possibility of the concept itself

However, we came upon it above from the side of its matter, from the concept of religion. We have yet, therefore, to attempt by means of a material discussion what we did not achieve by a formal one.

By the demonstrated untenability of this concept from the side of its form, everything that does not concern religion, from which alone it still awaits its confirmation, is at the same time excluded from its sphere, since nothing could previously be determined concerning the possible content of a revelation. We append to this concept, therefore, the further characteristic that what is made known in a revelation must be of religious content; and with this, then, the definition of this concept is completed.

§6

Material Discussion of the
Concept of Revelation
In Preparation for a Deduction of It[21]

All religious concepts can be derived only a priori from the postulates
of practical reason, as was demonstrated in §3 above by the actual
deduction of them. Now the concept of revelation is supposed to
have as its object a certain form of such concepts and cannot be
deduced from the side of its form (namely as concept); thus, if its
real possibility is to be secured, it can be deduced only from the side
of its content; and we have therefore to seek its origin in the field of
pure practical reason. It must be capable of deduction a priori from
ideas of this reason,[22] though certainly not without the presupposition
of all experience, yet solely with the presupposition of an [76]
experience in general, and certainly without having borrowed or
learned anything from it, but in order itself to prescribe the law for a
certain experience according to practical principles. This experience,
however, is not judged as an experience according to theoretical
laws but rather as an impetus in the determination of the will
according to practical laws, and it is a matter not of the correctness
or incorrectness of the observation made but rather of its practical
consequences. Here the case is not like the field of natural concepts,
where we can and must demonstrate in the deduction of a concept
a priori that without it either experience in general (if the concept is
pure) or a certain definite experience (if it is not pure) would not be
possible at all. Rather, since we are in the field of reason, we can
and may demonstrate only that without the origin of a certain
concept a priori no *rational acknowledgment* would be possible of
a certain experience as that which it gives itself out to be. This is all
the more necessary here, since this concept promises us who-knows-
what kind of knowledge in the field of the supersensuous by a
method that is already questionable in this regard, and threatens to

---

21 *Gesamtausgabe*, pp. 41–5 (§4). The opening lines (as far as note 22 below)
were added in the second edition, replacing a longer passage in the first
edition, which is translated in the Appendix, pp. 174–5 below.
22 See note 21 above.

open the door to every kind of fanaticism, unless it is a priori and we can thus prescribe laws for it, to which we can hold all of its possible a posteriori presumptions and limit them accordingly. It must therefore be demonstrated that *rationally* this concept is possible only a priori, and that it must thus acknowledge the laws of the principle through which it is possible. Otherwise, if this concept claims to prove its warrants completely and solely a posteriori, it must be demonstrated that it is completely false and surreptitious, and that its entire fate depends on this investigation. This investigation, therefore, is the main point of this critique.

Now even if we grant, however, that the possibility of its origin a priori, as an idea of reason, can be verified by a deduction, it still remains to be decided whether it is *given* a priori, or is *constructed* and *artificial*. And we admit that the peculiar way that it takes out of the world of ideas into the world of sense, and again out of the latter into the former, makes us at least suspect that it is the [77] latter. If this should be confirmed, then to begin with our preliminary judgment would hardly be favorable to it, since we already know that in the field of the supersensuous, reason may wander off into the infinite and dream. But from the fact that it was possible for reason to conceive something, it may not infer even the possibility that something in general might correspond to this idea. There still remains, however, one more way to lift this idea out of the empty dreams of reason. If, namely, a need can be demonstrated in experience, and specifically (since we are concerned here with a practical concept) an empirically given practical need, it would not, of course, give that concept a posteriori (which was certainly not given a priori), but it would nevertheless *justify* it. This experience, then, supplies what was lacking in the legitimacy of this concept a priori; it delivers the missing datum. Now it still does not follow from this that the concept itself is a posteriori, but only that it cannot be demonstrated a priori whether or not it is completely empty in general.

This limitation also determines the true character of the deduction of this concept a priori. It is not to be proved by this deduction, namely, that the concept is *actual* a priori, but only that it is *possible* a priori; not that every rational mind *must* necessarily possess it a priori, but that it *may* possess it, if its train of ideas tends more or less in this direction. The former would be possible only if a datum of pure reason could be pointed out a priori which compelled reason to arrive at this concept – as in the case, for example, of the idea of God, of the absolute totality of the world, etc., where the necessary task of reason was to seek the absolutely unconditioned for everything conditioned. But since such a datum is not to be found a priori, its deduction may and can demonstrate only its possibility as *idea*, and only insofar as it is idea.

Therefore, no historical* deduction of the origin of this concept among men would contradict this deduction, however probable [78] it might make it that the concept first arose through actual facts in the world of sense which were ascribed to supernatural causes out of ignorance or by willful deceit; not even an irrefutable proof that without this empirically given need no rational mind would ever have come upon this idea (if such a proof were possible) would contradict this deduction. For in the first case the concept *in concreto* would certainly have arisen quite illegitimately, which, however, cannot prejudice in the least the possibility of conceiving a legitimate origin of it *in abstracto*. In the second case, that empirical datum would surely have been the *incidental cause* of coming upon it; but provided that the concept is not determined by the *content* of the experience (and a deduction a priori should demonstrate the impossibility of this), it would not have been its principle. The *validity* of this concept is another matter, i.e., whether it can rationally be assumed that something outside us will correspond to it; this can certainly be deduced only empirically and thus extends no further than the validity of the datum from which it is deduced. Let us illustrate this by an example.

The concept of a fundamental evil principle alongside a good one is obviously an a priori concept, for it cannot be given in any experience; specifically, it is an idea of reason. And it must therefore be capable of deduction, according to its possibility, unless it completely contradicts rational principles. But this idea is not given a priori, but is rather constructed, since no datum of pure reason can be adduced for it. In experience, however, several data are found which seem to justify this concept and which could have been the incidental causes of its origin. Now if only these data actually justified it; if only people had wanted to employ it for a

---

* In general, all of those who *refute* the critical philosophy by historical, geographical, or physical deductions have not yet comprehended the first proposition of the philosophy which they refute. [Note added in the second edition.]

practical, though empirically conditioned, need and not solely for the theoretical explanation of nature; if only, finally, it did not completely contradict practical reason – then one would indeed have been permitted to assume it, at least as an idea to which [79] something *might* correspond, in spite of the fact that its validity appeals only to empirical data.

By the first deduction of the possibility of the concept of revelation a priori, then, not much appears to have been accomplished; and it cannot be denied that it would be a very empty and useless endeavor if it could not be demonstrated that this concept, if it is not possible a priori, is not rational at all. Consequently, its entire worth depends on this [latter] deduction.

Deduction of the Concept of Revelation
From A Priori Principles
Of Pure Reason[23]

If finite moral beings, i.e., beings who besides the moral law stand also under natural laws, are conceived as given, it can be presumed that the effects of these two causalities, whose laws are mutually quite independent of each other in determining the wills of such beings, will come into conflict, since the moral law is supposed to exercise its causality not merely in that part of these beings which stands immediately and solely under its legislation (their higher faculty of desire) but also in that part which stands first of all under natural laws. This conflict of the natural law with the moral law can be very different in strength according to the particular constitution of their sensuous nature, and a degree of this strength can be conceived in which the moral law wholly loses its causality in their sensuous nature, either forever or just in certain cases. Now if such beings are not to become wholly incapable of morality in this case, their sensuous nature itself must be determined by sensuous stimuli to let itself be determined by the moral law. If this is not to be a contradiction – and it certainly is one in itself to want to employ *sensuous* stimuli as determining grounds for *pure morality* – then it can only mean that pure moral stimuli are to be brought to [80] them by way of the senses. The only purely moral stimulus is the inward holiness of right. This has been presented *in concreto* (hence accessible to sensibility) in God by means of a postulate of pure practical reason, and he himself has been presented as moral judge of all rational beings according to this law given by *his* reason – hence as lawgiver to those beings. Now this idea of the will of the Most Holy as the moral law for all moral beings is, on the one hand, completely identical with the concept of the inward holiness of right and is therefore that single purely moral stimulus; and, on the other hand, it is capable of being the vehicle of the senses. This idea

---

[23] *Gesamtausgabe*, pp. 45–51 (§5). A lengthy passage at the beginning of this chapter in the first edition, which was omitted in the second, is translated in the Appendix, pp. 175–6 below.

alone, therefore, is adequate for the problem to be solved. No being is capable, however, of making this idea reach them by way of their sensuous nature; or, if it is already consciously present in them, capable of confirming it by the same way – no being except a lawgiver for this [sensuous] nature, who is then also, according to the postulates of practical reason, that moral lawgiver for finite rational beings. God himself, therefore, would have to proclaim to them, in the world of sense, both himself and his will to be lawful for them. The sensuous world in general, however, is so far from containing a proclamation of lawgiving holiness that we are unable to infer from it anything supernatural at all by means of the concepts applicable to it. And although we can infer this legislation by combining the concept of freedom with these concepts and with the concept of a final moral purpose for the world that is thereby possible (§4), this inference nevertheless already presupposes a causality of the moral law in the inferring subject – a causality which has effected not only the complete consciousness of its commandment that is possible only according to natural laws, but also the constant will to increase its efficacy in oneself by freely searching for and using every means, but which has not been assumed by the sensuously conditioned beings presupposed. God would therefore have to proclaim himself as lawgiver by means of a special appearance in the world of sense, determined expressly for this purpose and for these beings. Since God is determined by the moral law to promote [81] the highest possible morality in all rational beings by every moral means, it is to be expected, if such beings should really exist, that he would avail himself of this means if it is physically possible.*

This deduction accomplishes what it promised. The concept deduced is actually the concept of *revelation*, i.e., the concept of an appearance effected in the sensuous world by the causality of God, through which he proclaims himself as moral lawgiver. It is deduced from sheer a priori concepts of pure practical reason; from the causality of the moral law, which is required utterly and without any condition in all rational beings; from the single pure motive

---

* Surely no reader who has even the dimmest notion of the course and goal of this treatise needs to be reminded that an *objective* validity, grounding a theoretical proof a priori, is by no means to be ascribed to this deduction, but merely a *subjective* validity, sufficient for empirically conditioned faith – not even if someone should deliberately misconstrue its sense in order to lead the reader astray. [Note added in the second edition.]

of this causality, the inward holiness of right; from the concept of
God, which is to be assumed as real for the possibility of the required
causality, and from his determinations. From this deduction there
follows immediately the warrant for subjecting every alleged revelation – i.e., every appearance in the sensuous world that is to be
conceived as corresponding to this concept – to a critique of reason.
For if it is simply not possible to get the concept of revelation a
posteriori through the given appearance, but if rather the concept
itself is there a priori and only awaits an appearance corresponding
to it, then it is clearly a matter for reason to decide whether or not
this given appearance agrees with reason's concept of it. And reason
is accordingly so far from awaiting the law from revelation that she
rather prescribes it for herself. Furthermore, from reason must
follow all conditions under which an appearance can be accepted as
divine revelation; namely, it can be accepted only insofar as it [82]
agrees with this deduced concept. We call these conditions criteria
of the divinity of a revelation. So everything that is laid down as
such a criterion must be derivable from this deduction, and everything that is derivable from it is such a criterion.

But this deduction also does not accomplish any more than it
promised. The concept to be deduced was proclaimed merely as an
idea; the deduction can thus prove no objective validity for the
concept, whatever remarkable proof it might succeed in producing.
All that is required of it is to demonstrate that the concept to be
deduced contradicts neither itself nor one of the principles that it
must presuppose. Furthermore, it proclaims itself not as given but
rather as constructed (*conceptus not datus, sed ratiocinatus*); it has,
therefore, no datum of pure reason to exhibit by which it might be
given to us, and neither has it pretended to accomplish this.
Provisionally, then, it follows from these two determinations that if
ever an appearance should be given in the world of sense which
perfectly agrees with this concept (a revelation that would possess
all the criteria of divinity), one could nevertheless assert neither an
objective validity for this appearance, nor even a subjective validity
for all rational beings, but rather the actual acceptance of it as such
would still have to conform to other conditions. The datum for this
concept, missing from pure reason and possible only in experience –
namely, that moral beings are given who would be incapable of
morality without revelation – is presupposed as a hypothesis; and a
deduction of the concept of revelation does not have to prove its

actuality, which at any rate it could not accomplish for an empirical datum as a deduction a priori, but rather it is quite sufficient for it if only this presupposition does not contradict itself and is accordingly perfectly conceivable. But precisely because this datum is expected only from experience, this concept is not purely a priori. The physical possibility of an appearance corresponding to this [83] concept cannot be proved by a deduction of it, which is conducted only from principles of practical, not theoretical, reason; rather, it must be presupposed. Its moral possibility is simply required for the possibility of its concept and follows in general from the possibility of the above deduction. But whether or not a revelation given *in concreto* contradicts this requirement is the business of an applied critique of this given revelation; and the conditions under which it would not contradict it is the business of a critique of the concept of revelation in general.

From everything that has been said up to this point, the further course of our investigation also becomes clear. The possibility of this concept, insofar as it is such, i.e., its conceivability, has been demonstrated. Whether it might not be altogether empty, however, or whether something corresponding to it could be expected from a rational point of view, depends on the empirical possibility (not the mere conceivability) of the empirical datum presupposed in it as a condition. So this is what must be proved before everything else. But a critique of all revelation also has to prove nothing more in regard to this datum than its absolute possibility, whereas the critique of an alleged revelation *in concreto* would have to show the definite actuality of the presupposed empirical need, as can be further established only in what follows.

It is not necessary to prove that an appearance in the sensuous world in general, effected by freedom according to a concept of purpose – hence also a revelation – could be conceived as physically possible, since it has already been assumed in order to make possible the absolutely required causality of the moral law upon the sensuous world. We will nevertheless undertake some investigations concerning this physical possibility by way of explanation, not of proof, and because of some important consequences issuing from it for the rectification of the concept of revelation.

With the conclusion of these two investigations, it must be fully clear whether from a rational point of view something [84] corresponding to the concept of revelation could be expected or not.

In order to make possible, however, the application of this concept to a particular appearance given *in concreto*, a more precise analysis is still needed of the concept of revelation itself, which is to be applied. The conditions under which such an application is possible must all be in the concept and be capable of development from it by means of an analysis of it. They are called criteria. Our next business after these investigations will therefore be to establish and to prove these criteria.

By this means, then, the possibility will be fully secured not only of expecting for this concept in general something corresponding to it, but also of applying it to an actually given appearance. But even if such an application is fully possible, we are still unable to recognize any reason why we ought to make it actual. Only after showing such a reason, therefore, is the critique of all revelation concluded.

§8

The Possibility of the Empirical Datum
Presupposed in the Concept of Revelation[24]

The experience presupposed in the deduction of the concept of revelation from a priori practical principles of reason is this: there could be moral beings in which the moral law loses its causality *for ever*, or only *in certain cases*. The moral law exerts a causality on the higher faculty of desire for the determination of the will; by this means it exerts a causality on the lower faculty in order to produce the complete freedom of the moral subject from the coercion of natural impulses. If the first kind of causality is suspended, the *will* fails to acknowledge any law at all and to be obedient to it; if only the second kind is hindered, then with all good will man is too weak *really to practice* the good that he wills. The empirical possibility of this hypothesis is to be proved – i.e., it is to be demonstrated, [85] not from the arrangement of human nature in general insofar as it is to be cognized generally and a priori, but rather from its empirical determinations, that it is possible and probable that the moral law might lose its causality in them. For thereby the question is answered: Why was a revelation needed, and why were human beings not able to help themselves with natural religion alone? The causes of it cannot lie in the arrangement of human nature in general, insofar as it is to be cognized a priori; for otherwise we would have to be able to demonstrate a priori the need of a revelation; a datum of pure reason would have to be adduced for this, and the concept of it would be a given one. Rather, its causes must lie in contingent determinations of human nature. But in order to discern fully the limits within which rational religion is sufficient, within which natural religion arises, and where revealed religion finally becomes necessary, it will be very useful to investigate the relationship of human nature to religion, in general as well as according to its particular determinations.

Man stands, as part of the world of sense, under natural laws. In respect to his faculty of cognition, he is obliged to progress from

[24] *Gesamtausgabe*, pp. 51–69 (§6).

intuitions, which stand under the laws of sensibility, to concepts; and in respect to his lower faculty of desire, to allow himself to be determined by sensuous stimuli. As a being of a supersensuous world, however, according to his rational nature, his higher faculty of desire is determined by a completely different law, and this law through its requirements reveals vistas of knowledge to him that stand neither under the conditions of intuition nor under those of concepts. But since his faculty of cognition is utterly bound to those conditions, and he can conceive of nothing at all without them, he is obliged also to place these objects of a supernatural world under those conditions, although he recognizes that such a manner of representation is only subjectively, not objectively, valid, and [86] that it entitles him neither to theoretical nor practical *conclusions*. His lower faculty of desire, determinable by sensuous stimuli, is subordinated to the higher, and it ought never to determine his will where duty speaks. This is an essential arrangement of human nature. So man *ought* to be, and so he is *able* to be, too; for everything that hinders him from being so is not essential to his nature but contingent and can therefore not only be thought nonexistent but can also actually be nonexistent. In what relationship does he now stand in this situation to religion? Does he need it? Which one? And for what purpose?

The next consequence of this original arrangement of human nature is that the moral law appears to him as a commandment and not as a statement; that it speaks to him of 'ought' and not of 'is'; that he is conscious of being *able* also to act differently than this law commands; that consequently, according to his representation, he receives a worth and a merit whenever he so acts. This worth, which he gives to himself, entitles him to expect the Happiness appropriate to it. However, he cannot give the latter to himself like the former; he therefore expects it from the supreme executor of the law, who is proclaimed to him by the law. This being attracts his entire reverence because He has an eternal worth, compared with which his own worth disappears into nothing, and attracts his entire affection because he expects from Him all the good that he has to expect. He cannot remain indifferent before the ever-present Observer, Watchman, and Judge of his most secret thoughts, and the most just Recompenser thereof. He must wish to manifest to Him his admiration and reverence, and to do it, since he can do it in no other way, through strict obedience performed *with regard to Him*.

This is pure rational religion. Religiousness of this kind does not expect from the thought of the lawgiver an impetus to facilitate the determination of the will but only satisfaction of its need to show its affection for him. It expects no requirement from God to obey him but only the permission in its willing obedience to [87] look upon him. It does not want to do God a favor by serving him; rather, it expects from him as the highest grace that he allow himself to be served by it.

This is the highest moral perfection of man. It presupposes not only the firm will always to act morally but also complete freedom. It is impossible a priori to determine whether any *human being* is capable of this moral perfection *in concreto*, and in the present situation of mankind it is not at all probable.

The second degree of moral goodness presupposes this same firm will to obey the moral law altogether but not complete freedom in individual cases. The sensuous inclination still struggles against the feeling of duty and is just as often victor as vanquished. The causes of this moral weakness lie not in the essential elements of human nature, but rather are contingent: in part, in the case of this or that subject, a bodily constitution that favors the greater intensity and more lasting duration of the passions; in part, and primarily, the present situation of humanity, in which we become accustomed to act according to natural impulses much earlier than according to moral grounds, and in which we get into the situation where we must be determined by the former much more often than by the latter, so that our development as natural men almost always has great advantages over our moral formation. Since the serious will to act morally – hence a lively, active, moral feeling – is presupposed in this state of affairs, this weakness must be very unpleasant for man, and he must eagerly search out and make use of every means to facilitate his determination by the moral law. If it is thus a matter of securing the predominance of the moral over the sensuous inclination, this can happen in two ways: partly by weakening the sensuous inclination and partly by strengthening the stimulus of the moral law, the respect for it. The first takes place according to technico-practical rules, which are based on natural principles, [88] and about which everyone must be instructed by his own reflection, experience, and self-knowledge. They lie outside the sphere of our present investigation. The stimulus of the moral law can be strengthened in no other way, without damaging morality, than through vivid representation of the inner nobility and holiness of its demands – through an urgent feeling of 'ought' and 'must.' And how can this become more urgent than when we have constantly in mind the representation of a completely holy being who commands us to be holy? In him we perceive agreement with the law no longer merely as something that *ought* to be but as something that *is*; in him we see presented the necessity of such a state of affairs. How better can the moral feeling be strengthened than through the representation that in acting immorally not merely do we despise ourselves, we who are imperfect beings – no, that the supreme Perfection must despise us? How better than through the representation that in overcoming ourselves and sacrificing our dearest inclinations for duty, not only do we honor ourselves, but essential Holiness must honor us? How can we become more attentive to the voice of our conscience and quicker to learn from it than when we hear in it the voice of the Most Holy, who always accompanies us invisibly and espies the most secret thoughts of our heart – *before whom we walk*?[25] Since the inclination in the subject struggles against this new impetus of the moral law that does it damage, reason will seek to fortify it by completely securing the ground on which it rests. Reason will seek a proof for the concept of God as moral lawgiver, and it will find it in the concept of God as creator of the world. This is the second degree of moral perfection, which establishes natural religion.

This religion should, of course, become a means for determining the will in particular cases where the struggle of inclination against duty occurs. However, it presupposes that the first and highest determination of the will – to obey the moral law in general – has already taken place through the moral law; for this religion does not present itself but must rather be sought, and no one can [89] seek it who does not wish it.

Finally, the most extreme corruption of rational beings with regard to morality is when there is not even the will to acknowledge a moral law and to obey it, when sensuous impulses are the only determining grounds of their faculty of desire. It appears, first of all at least, to prove nothing at all for the necessity of a revelation even if one were able to show in society among other, morally better men ever so many subjects depraved to this extent.

[25] An allusion to biblical, especially Old Testament, language – e.g., Gen. 24.40; 48.15; Ps. 56.13; 116.9.

For it must be possible for the better ones, and it is their duty (one might say) to develop moral feeling in the worse ones through teaching and training and thus to lead them to the need for a religion. Without engaging in this investigation for the present, we want to put the question only in such a way that its answer becomes decisive for the demonstration of an empirical need for revelation: was it possible that all humanity, or at least whole regions of peoples and lands, could fall into this extreme moral corruption? In order to be able to answer it, we must first define the concept of empirical sensibility somewhat more precisely.

Sensibility in general (that is, empirical sensibility) could be appropriately described as an inability to represent ideas, since this description includes simultaneously the theoretical error of being able to conceive of ideas either not at all or in no way except under the conditions of empirical sensibility, and the practical one, which follows necessarily from the first, of not letting oneself be determined by ideas. One can divide empirical, just like pure, sensibility into two classes, *external* and *internal*. The first, in its theoretical respect, consists in conceiving of everything under the empirical conditions of the external senses – audibly, tangibly, visibly, etc. – and also in wanting actually to see, hear, and feel everything; and this is always associated with an utter inability to reflect, to follow a series of inferences, even when it concerns only objects of [90] nature. And in its practical respect it consists in allowing oneself to be determined only by the pleasure of external sense. This degree of sensibility is the same as what is also termed 'gross sensibility.' The second class, in its theoretical respect, consists in conceiving of everything as modifiable – at least everything under the empirical conditions of our inner sense – and also in wanting actually to modify it. And in its practical respect it consists in allowing oneself to be determined by nothing higher than the pleasure of inner sense. To this class belongs the pleasure in play, in poetry, in the beautiful (but not in the sublime), even in reflection, in the feeling of one's power, and even sympathy, although it is the noblest of all sensuous impulses. When this sensibility is dominant, i.e., when we allow ourselves to be determined solely and simply by its stimulus and never by the moral law, then it is clear that it totally excludes all will to be good and all morality. But certainly in most human beings it predominates by far, and in most cases they are determined solely by it; but nevertheless they are not therefore incapable of all purely moral acts in general and still have at least enough moral feeling to feel the culpability and indecency of their manner of acting in conspicuous cases or on certain occasions and to be ashamed of it. Even supposing, however, that they never applied the moral law to themselves and never felt shame or remorse over their own imperfection, it would become evident nevertheless in their judging of the acts of others, in their often strong disapproval of them on genuinely moral grounds, that they are not totally incapable of moral sense. One would have an effect on men of this kind, one should think, precisely at the point where they still show sensitivity for morality: one would be able to make use of just those principles which they apply to others in order to open their eyes to their own condition, and thus to lead them gradually to good will and through it finally to religiousness. In order to show the necessity of a revelation, [91] then, one would have to be able to show that human beings, and whole races of human beings, are possible who through dominant sensibility have been deprived of the sense for morality either wholly, or to so great a degree that one could not influence them at all in this way – who are either not conscious of the moral law in themselves at all, or else so little that one could build nothing at all in them on this basis. It can certainly be conceived a priori that mankind could have come into a situation, either from its origins or through various fortunes, such that it was compelled in continual, hard struggle with nature for its subsistence to direct all its thoughts continually to what was in front of its nose, to be able to think of nothing but the present, and to be able to hear no other law than that of need. In such a situation it is impossible for moral feeling to awaken and ethical concepts to evolve. But mankind will not always remain in this situation; except in special cases it will not remain so for long. With the help of experience it will make rules for itself and will abstract maxims for its behavior. These maxims, arising merely through experience in nature, will likewise be applied only to such experience and will often contradict possible moral rules. Nevertheless, proven by their applicability and by general precedent, they will be transmitted from generation to generation and augmented; and now it will be they that destroy the possibility of morality, after that urgent need, which did the same before them, has been partially removed by them. If one considers the inhabitants of Tierra del Fuego, who pass their life in a condition that borders so nearly on animality; the majority of the inhabitants of the South Sea islands, for whom theft seems to be quite a matter of indifference and of which they seem not to be ashamed in the least; those negroes who without much hesitation sell their wife or their children into slavery for a drink of brandy[26] – if one considers such examples, one appears to find the first observation confirmed in experience; and in order to be convinced [92] of the correctness of the second, one has only to study the customs and maxims of politicized peoples.

How, then, is mankind to get from this condition to morality, and through it to religion? Cannot man find it by himself? In order to answer this question more definitely, we must compare what is here being presupposed with mankind's condition. In order to decide whether or not a people in its present condition is capable of morality in general, it is not enough to consider its behavior; and the conclusion is premature that a certain people, generally and without a trace of the slightest shame, commits acts which conflict with the first principles of all morality, and that it is therefore without all moral feeling. One must investigate whether even just the concept of duty in general does not appear among them, however obscurely conceived. And if one then finds there, for example, only this much – that they trust in the observance of a contract which they are not able to enforce, even in the case where it would be advantageous to the other party not to keep it, and that they risk this trust; that in the case of its violation they display more active and bitter indignation than they would display about the harm thereby inflicted on themselves – if one finds only this much, then one must concede to them the concept of duty in general. But without this trust in the observance of contracts, it is not even possible to be united to society. That people, then, which merely lives in social union is not without all moral sense. Unfortunately, however, it is the general habit of all those in whom sensibility is dominant to make use of this feeling, not also as the ground for determining their own actions, but rather solely and simply as the principle for judging the actions of others. Indeed, they go so far, especially when sensibility is already reduced to maxims, as to deem a sacrifice, a denial of self-interest for duty, to be ridiculous folly and to be

---

26 In the first edition Fichte included one further item in this series of examples: '... all those peoples that a man of famous name accuses of such a deplorable vacuity of virtue that he even believes himself expressly justified in assigning to them a separate class in the human race...'

ashamed of it; and thus to regard themselves always and ever as standing merely under the natural concept. Finally, they even [93] behave so consistently as to give precisely the same credit to the other person, provided that they themselves do not have a personal stake in it and that their own interests are not injured by the other person's violation of duty. Only in the latter case do they remember that there are duties; and this, then, makes the development of this concept very questionable whenever we come across it combined with dominant sensibility and justifies us in believing that merely the principle of the latter, that of self-interest, has given rise to it. So even the will to be morally good is not to be combined with dominant sensibility. But since this will is unavoidably necessary for *seeking* a religion as means for a stronger determination by the moral law, mankind in this condition can never find a religion by itself, for it is not able even to seek one.

And even if it were able to seek one, it is not able to *find* one. In order to be convinced in the manner developed above that it is God who speaks to us through the moral law, one first of all needs the concept of a creation of the world by a cause outside it. Mankind, even those men who are still very uneducated, will easily arrive at this concept. Man is compelled a priori to conceive an absolute totality of conditions; and he merely concludes the series of them sooner and faster the less he is educated and the more incapable he is of following a long series. Hence, among persons of crude sensibility everything will be full of belief in supernatural causes, in daemons without number. A more educated sensibility will raise itself perhaps to the concept of a single first cause, an ingenious architect of the world. For the purpose of a religion, however, we do not need this concept but rather that of a *moral* creator of the world, and in order to attain it we need the concept of a final moral purpose of the world. Now sensibility, to be sure, will once again arrive easily at the concept of possible purposes in the world, because it is itself guided by the representation of purposes in its dealings here below; but the concept of a *final* moral *purpose* of creation is possible only for the educated moral feeling. The [94] merely sensuous man, therefore, will never arrive either at it, nor through it at the principle of a religion.

In the first place, if a means should nevertheless be devised to bring religion to him, what need does he have of it? The best moral man, who had not only the earnest will to obey the moral law but also complete freedom, needed it only to satisfy in some way the feeling of reverence and thankfulness towards the supreme being. The one who had likewise the earnest will but not complete freedom needed it in order to add a new impetus to the authority of the moral law which would counterbalance the strength of the inclination and bring about freedom. The one who does not even have the will to acknowledge a moral law and to obey it needs it just to produce this will in himself in the first place and by means of it to produce freedom. With him, therefore, religion has to take a wholly different way. Pure rational religion as well as natural religion are based on moral feeling; revealed religion, on the other hand, is itself supposed to establish moral feeling in the first place. The first [type of religion] found no resistance at all but found rather all the inclinations in the subject prepared to accept it. The second had to combat the inclinations only in particular cases but came on the whole as something desired and sought. The last has to counterbalance not only all immoral inclinations but even complete opposition to acknowledging a law in general and antipathy towards itself for wanting to make the law valid. This religion, therefore, can and will make use of weightier motives so far as this can be done without impairing freedom, i.e., without acting against its own purpose.

By what way, then, can this religion reach men so constituted? Naturally, by precisely the same way that everything which they conceive or by which they let themselves be determined reaches them: by way of sensibility. God must announce himself to them directly through the senses; he must demand obedience from [95] them directly through the senses.

But here two cases are still possible. Either, God develops the moral feeling by the process of reflection through a supernatural effect in the world of sense in the heart of one or of several, whom he has chosen to be his mediators to mankind, and by the same process builds upon this feeling the principle of all religion, with the command to do to the rest of mankind just what he has done to them. Or, he proclaims this principle directly and bases it on his authority as Lord. In the first case we would not even be compelled to assume God to be the immediate cause of this supernatural effect; rather, although we have assumed a general moral corruption of mankind, yet one of the possible higher moral beings could quite suitably be the cause of such an effect. But if we find grounds from some other quarter for positing the ground of such an effect immediately in God, we will not at all invalidate these grounds if we say that it is improper to make God the pedagogue; for according to our knowledge of God, nothing is improper for him except what is against the moral law. Then in this case, too – without investigating which moral being may be the motivating cause of this development – we would not have a revelation but rather a natural religion brought to us by a supernatural process. If this means had only been possible and sufficient to achieve the purpose, then no revelation would have been necessary, i.e., no proclamation of God as lawgiver grounded *directly* on God's authority. Let us assume for a moment that God wishes to make use of this means. He will doubtless produce the anticipated rational conviction in the souls of those on whom he acts. In conformity with his commands and their own feeling of obligation to propagate morality further, they will turn to the rest of mankind and seek to build up in them this same conviction by the same process by which it was built up in [96] them. There is no reason, either in human nature in general or in the empirical constitution of the assumed persons in particular, why it should be impossible for these delegates to achieve their purpose if only they find a hearing, if only they can secure attention. But how will they obtain it from persons who must already be prejudiced against the result of their representation in advance? What will they give these persons who shun reflection so that they will take the trouble of reflecting in order to be forced to recognize the truth of a religion that wants to curb their inclinations and bring them under a law? Only the last case, therefore, remains: they must proclaim their doctrines on divine authority, and as his emissaries to mankind.

This, too, appears to be possible in two different ways: either God also grounds the faith of these his emissaries simply on authority; or he wishes, and expects from their own insight, only that they proclaim to the rest of mankind on divine authority what has been developed out of their heart through the simple process of reflection by whatever means, insofar as they realize that no other means remains for bringing religion to them. This last way, however, is impossible; for in that case God would have willed that these his delegates – though with the most salutary intention, to be sure – should lie and deceive. Lying and deceit, however, with whatever intention it may be done, always remains wrong, because it can never become the principle of a universal legislation; and God can never will something wrong.

Finally, one could conceive as yet a third possibility that God has willed that these allegedly inspired ones should deceive themselves and ascribe to a supernatural cause a proclamation of the divine moral legislation based on authority, which had arisen in themselves quite naturally, e.g., through their fantasy being stimulated by the wish for it. Any categorical answer to this question, in the affirmative as well as the negative, could be based solely on [97] theoretical principles, because it is a question of explaining a natural appearance according to such laws. All of natural philosophy, however, does not extend so far as to prove that something in the world of sense is possible *only* through laws of nature, or that it is *not* possible through them. Therefore, this assertion, applied to the discussion of a revelation *in concreto*, can never be either proved or refuted; neither does it belong, however, in the investigation of the possible origin of a revealed religion, which is undertaken solely from practical principles. To be sure, a certain effect, regarded as a natural appearance, might have arisen from natural laws discoverable by us; and at the same time it might nevertheless be very appropriate to the concept of a rational being for us to ascribe it to a supernatural cause, at least until the achievement of its moral intent. And so the following disjunctive proposition is not nearly sufficient to ground the categorical assertion at which it aims: certain allegedly inspired persons were either actually inspired, or they were deceivers, or they were fanatics (expressed more correctly and mildly, they were imperfect natural scientists). For, in the first place, the concepts that are placed alongside each other as terms of the classification do not invalidate one another. The possibility of accepting the last one must be refuted or proved from natural concepts; the possibility of the first two, however, can only be demonstrated from practical principles. But these two principles do not affect one another, and what one denies can very well be affirmed from the other. Thus the last case and one of the first two are possible simultaneously; only the first two are contradictory. In the second place, the impossibility of the last one can never be demonstrated in a given case. But all of this will receive its full clarity only in what follows, where we will talk about the physical possibility of the anticipated supernatural effect in the world of sense.

Therefore, since the possibility of the latter case, which we certainly cannot remove, must not lead us astray, we can now [98] safely draw the following results from all we have proved until now: mankind can fall so deep into moral corruption that it can be brought back to morality in no other way than by religion, and to religion in no other way than by the senses. A religion that is to affect such men can be based on nothing but direct divine authority. Since God cannot will that any moral being should fabricate such an authority, he must himself be the one who confers it on such a religion.

But for what purpose, then, is this authority? And what can God base it on when he has to do with men who are sensuous to this degree? Plainly not on a nobility for which they have no sense and no reverence, nor on his holiness, which would already presuppose in them the moral feeling that is first to be developed by religion; but rather on that for whose admiration they are receptive on natural grounds: on his greatness and might as Lord of nature and as their Lord. It is heteronomy, however, and does not bring about morality but at most enforces legality to behave in accordance with the moral law only because a superior being wills it; and a religion based on this authority would consequently contradict itself. But this authority is not even supposed to ground obedience; it is supposed to ground only attention to the motives for obedience, which are to be displayed subsequently. Attention, however, as an empirical determination of our soul, is to be aroused by natural means. Of course, it would be plainly contradictory to want to force even just this attention through fear of threatened punishments by this powerful being, or even through physical means; or to want to obtain it insidiously through promised rewards: contradictory, because fear and hope sooner distract attention than arouse it and can at most produce only a mechanical repetition but not conviction based on rational deliberation, which must alone be the basis of all morality; contradictory, because it would falsify the principle of all [99] religion at the very beginning and present God as a being to whom one could make oneself pleasing by something other than moral attitudes – here, by listening unwillingly to things in which one has no interest and scrupulously repeating them. But the representation of ever so great a might also excites, so long as we do not think of ourselves in opposition to it, not fear but rather admiration and devotion, which of course rests only on emotional and not moral grounds, but which powerfully attracts our attention to everything that comes from the mighty being. So long as God does not proclaim himself as moral lawgiver but merely as a speaking person, we do not yet think of ourselves in opposition to him; and when he does proclaim himself as such, he proclaims his holiness to us simultaneously, which takes away from us all possible fear of his might, since it assures us that he will never make arbitrary use of it against us but that its effects on us will depend entirely on ourselves. God's requirement in a possible revelation that we *listen* to him is based, therefore, on his omnipotence and eternal greatness and can be based on nothing else, since beings who need a revelation are not capable in the first place of any other representation of him. His requirement to *obey* him, however, can be based on nothing but his holiness, because otherwise the purpose of all revelation – to further pure morality – would not be achieved; but the concept of holiness as well as the devotion towards it must already have been developed through the revelation.

We have a sublime saying that illustrates this: Ye shall be holy, for I am holy, says the Lord.[27] The Lord speaks as Lord and thereby summons everything to attention. But he does not base the demand of holiness on this his lordship but rather on his own holiness.

But it will still be asked: How will these persons then judge, before their moral feeling has been awakened, whether it [100] might be God who speaks? And here we come to the answer to an objection that must already have been in the mind of every reader for some time. We have proved in the preceding chapter [§7] that from a rational point of view the concept of revelation is possible only a priori and could not legitimately arise a posteriori; and in the present chapter we have shown that there might be a condition – indeed, that the entire human race might fall into this condition – in which it is impossible for them to arrive a priori at the concept of religion, and so also of revelation. This is a formal contradiction, one may say; or one can exhibit the dilemma to us as follows: either, men already felt the moral need that was able to drive them to seek a religion and already had all moral concepts, which were able to convince them rationally of its truths; thus they needed no revelation but already had religion a priori. Or, they neither felt that need nor did they have those concepts; thus they were never able to convince themselves of the divinity of a religion on moral grounds; neither were they able to do so on theoretical grounds; they were unable, therefore, to do it at all, and a revelation is consequently impossible. But it does not follow that men who were not much

27 Cf. Lev. 11.44; 19.2; 1 Pet. 1.16.

aware of the moral commandment in themselves and could not be driven by it to the search for a religion – thus, who needed revelation – were not able subsequently to develop that feeling in themselves precisely with the help of this revelation, and thus to become capable of examining a revelation, and thus to investigate rationally whether or not it could be of divine origin. A doctrine was proclaimed to them as divine and thereby aroused at least their attention. Either, they now accepted it immediately as divine; and since they could neither infer this from theoretical principles nor investigate it according to moral ones – because until now their moral feeling was still undeveloped – they accepted something entirely without basis, and they were fortunate if the accident was useful to them. Or, they rejected it immediately, and thus they rejected something [101] again entirely without basis. Or, finally, they left the matter undecided until they should find rational grounds for judgment; and in this case alone did they act rationally. They could never prove *that* God speaks or *that* he does *not* speak (as a categorical assertion possible on theoretical grounds); whether he *could* have spoken could become clear only from the content of what was said in his name; they must therefore listen to it in the first place. If their moral feeling was then developed through this listening, then simultaneously there developed the concept of a religion and of its possible content, whether it comes to us through revelation or without it. And now in order to attain a rational assent, they were able and compelled to compare the revelation proclaimed to them as divine with the concept of a revelation a priori which they now had developed, and to pass judgment on it according to its agreement or nonagreement with this concept – which then fully resolves the supposed contradiction. A rational acceptance of a given revelation as divine is possible only on a priori grounds, but incidental causes can be given a posteriori – and must be in certain cases – for developing these grounds.

Now all these investigations have done more to prepare the actual point in question than to define it and develop it. That is to say, according to all that has been said until now, no rational acceptance of a revelation as divine takes place any sooner than after the complete development of moral feeling in us. Furthermore, every decision to obey a law of God can be based only on this feeling and the will to obey reason, which is thereby established in us (§3). Therefore, the divine authority on which a given revelation could be based appears to lose its entire utility as soon as it becomes possible to acknowledge it. That is, as long as such a revelation works to cultivate a receptivity to morality in a man, it is quite problematic for him whether it even might be of divine origin, because [102] this can result only from an evaluation of it according to moral principles; but as soon as such a judgment is possible, after the development of moral feeling in him has been accomplished, this moral feeling alone appears able to suffice for determining him to obey the moral law, simply as such. And, as was likewise shown above (§3), even with the firmest will to obey the moral law simply as the law of reason, particular cases are possible in which the law needs a strengthening of its causality through the representation that it is God's law. Nevertheless, the representation of this divine legislation is quite possible according to its matter through practical rational principles as well as according to its form through its application to the concept of a world; and there appears to be no reason why he should think of it as given by a supernatural effect in the world of sense. Thus, a need must be shown, though of course only an empirical one, which can be remedied only by the definite representation of a proclamation of God as moral lawgiver *which takes place through an effect in the world of sense*, if this entire representation is not to be in vain and the concept of a revelation empty, since a belief in it could at most be useful as long as it is not possible and would lose its entire utility as soon as it becomes possible. For we cannot possibly declare the pious sentiments about the goodness of God condescending to our weakness, and so forth, to be the total enduring utility of a revelation.

Now in the above deduction of the concept of revelation for the purpose of showing its real possibility, not only are rational beings presupposed in whom the moral law has lost its causality forever, but also those for whom it has happened in particular cases. Where there is not even the will to acknowledge a moral law and to obey it, the moral law is utterly without causality; where, on the [103] contrary, the will is there but not complete freedom, it loses its causality in particular cases. How revelation restores its efficacy in the first case has now been shown; now the question is whether also in the second case revelation has an influence that is essential to it and possible only by means of it. Since in the first case revelation cannot yet from a rational point of view be acknowledged as that which it claims to be, one could call this its function – the function of revelation *in itself*, insofar as it is wholly independent of our manner of representation, that is, according to its *matter* (*functio revelationis materialiter spectatae*). On the other hand, that which revelation would have to accomplish in the second case could be called the function of revelation insofar as we acknowledge it as such, that is, according to its *form* (*functio revelationis formaliter spectatae*); and, since revelation properly only becomes revelation by our recognizing it as such, one could call this the function of revelation *in the most proper sense*.

In the above discussion of the function of a revelation according to its matter, we quite rightly assumed that it relates only to subjects in whom there is not even the will to obey the rational law, and that, on the other hand, it does not have as its objects in this function those who do not lack this will but do lack complete freedom to carry it out, but rather that natural religion is sufficient to produce freedom in subjects of this sort. Now the determination of the will by the moral law is to be made possible through revelation by means of its first function, hence all rational beings are to be elevated to the second stage of moral perfection. For this reason, if natural religion could always be satisfying to beings at this second stage, no function at all of revelation according to its form could occur, and since this is the function of revelation in the most proper sense, no true need for a belief in revelation could be shown. But if it did occur, this appears to contradict the above proposition about [104] the sufficiency of natural religion to produce freedom. Therefore, we have to investigate in the first place whether it is possible to conceive of the representation that a revelation has occurred as influencing the mind to restore the arrested freedom of the will, and then, if such an influence should be shown, to investigate whether and to what extent the two assertions can be compatible.

It is one of the peculiarities of the empirical character of man that as long as one of his mental powers is particularly excited and in lively activity others are inactive and, as it were, enervated – and all the more so, the farther removed they are from the active one; and their enervation is greater, the greater its activity. Thus, one would strive in vain to determine someone differently by rational grounds who is determined by sensuous attraction or is in an intense emotional state. It is just as certain, on the other hand, that an elevation of the soul through ideas or its exertion through reflection is possible during which sensuous impressions lose almost their entire power. If a person is to be affected in such cases, it can happen in almost no other way than by means of that power which is in activity right now, since hardly an impression can be made on the others; or even if it could be made, it would not be sufficient to determine the person's will.

Some mental powers have a closer relationship and a greater reciprocal influence on each other than do others. One will try in vain through rational grounds to restrain the person who is carried away by sensuous attraction, but by presenting another sensuous impression by means of the imagination it can very easily succeed without the sensuous object being present, thus without direct sensation. All powers determinable by empirical sensibility stand in such correspondence.

The determinations antagonistic to duty are all caused by impressions on these powers: by a sensation which either corresponds directly to the object outside us or is reproduced by the [105] empirical imagination; by emotional states; by passions. What is the person to use, then, to counterbalance such a determination, when it is so strong that it completely suppresses the voice of reason? Obviously this counterweight must be brought to the soul by a power of the mind which on the one hand is sensuous, and is thus capable of working against a determination of the sensuous nature of the person, and which on the other hand is determinable through freedom and has spontaneity. And this power of the mind is the imagination. So by this means the only possible motive for a morality, the representation of the legislation of the Holy One, must be brought to the soul. Now this representation is based on principles of reason in natural religion; but if this reason, as we are presupposing, is completely suppressed, its results appear dim, uncertain, unreliable. Even the principles of this representation, therefore, should be capable of representation by the imagination. Now principles of this kind would be facts in the world of sense, or a revelation. The person in such moments must be able to say, 'God is, for he has spoken and acted; he wills that I now do not act in this way, for he has forbidden it expressly, with such-and-such words, under such-and-such circumstances, etc.; I shall one day answer to him amid certain appointed ceremonies for the resolution that I shall now make.' If such representations are to make an impression on him, however, he must be able to accept the facts underlying them as fully true and correct; so they must not perchance be fabricated by his own power of imagination but must rather be given to it. It follows immediately from our presupposition that such a representation of pure morality does not prejudice an action caused by it. The impetus presented sensuously by the imagination should be none other than the holiness of the lawgiver, and only its vehicle should be sensuous.

A general critique of the concept of revelation does not properly have to investigate whether meanwhile the purity of the motive does not often suffer by means of the sensibility of the [106] vehicle, and whether fear of punishment or hope of reward does not often have far more influence on an obedience caused by the representation of revelation than pure respect for the holiness of the lawgiver. A general critique, rather, has only to prove that this is not necessary *in abstracto,* and that *in concreto* it simply must not happen if religiousness is to be genuine and not merely more refined selfishness. Meanwhile, this can happen only too easily. Furthermore, it cannot be shown in general when, to what extent, and why such a strengthening of the moral law through the representation of a revelation is necessary at all. Finally, it is simply not to be denied that there is a universal drive in us, based unquestionably on the moral law, to honor a rational being more, the less the idea of absolute right in his mind needs strengthening in order to move him to produce it. For these reasons, it also cannot be denied that it would be far more honorable for mankind if natural religion were always sufficient to determine men in every case to obedience of the moral law. And in this sense, then, the two propositions can indeed be compatible: namely, that [1] it cannot be perceived a priori (before the actual experience) why the representation of a revelation should be necessary in order to restore the arrested freedom; but that [2] the nearly universal experience in ourselves and others teaches us almost daily that we are indeed weak enough to have need of a representation of this sort.

§9

The Physical Possibility of a Revelation[28]

The a priori concept of revelation, as justified by showing a need of empirical sensibility a posteriori, anticipates a supernatural effect in the world of sense. But one might ask in this connection: Is this even possible in general? Is it conceivable in general that something *outside* nature would have a causality *within* nature? And we will answer this question, partly in order to bring somewhat more light if possible, at least for our present purpose, to the still obscure [107] teaching about the possible compatibility of necessity according to natural laws and freedom according to moral laws; and partly in order to derive from the discussion of this question a consequence not unimportant for the rectification of the concept of revelation.

That it must be possible in general is the first postulate that practical reason makes a priori, by determining the supernatural in us, our higher faculty of desire, to become a cause outside itself in the world of sense, either of the one within us or the one outside us, which is here the same.

It must be remembered in the first place, however, that it is one thing to say that the will, as the higher faculty of desire, is free; for if this means what it says – that the will does not stand under natural laws – then it is immediately plausible, because the will, as higher faculty, is not a part of nature at all but rather something super-sensuous. But it is quite another thing to say that such a determination of the will becomes a causality in the world of sense, in which case we require, of course, that something standing under natural laws should be determined by something that is not a part of nature, which appears to be contradictory and to annul the concept of natural necessity, which after all makes possible the concept of a nature in general in the first place.

At this point we need first of all to recall that as long as we are talking only about explanation of nature, we are absolutely not allowed to assume a causality through freedom, because the whole

28 *Gesamtausgabe*, pp. 69–74 (§7).

of natural philosophy knows nothing of any such causality. And, on the other hand, as long as we are talking only about determination of the higher faculty of desire, it is simply not necessary to take into account the existence of a nature at all. The two causalities, that of the natural and that of the moral law, are infinitely different, according not only to the manner of their causality but also to their objects. The natural law commands with absolute necessity; the moral law commands freedom. The former governs nature; the latter the world of the spirit. The watchword of the former, *must*, and the watchword of the latter, *ought*, speak of completely different [108] things and cannot contradict each other, even if opposed, for they do not meet.

Their effects in the world of sense, however, do meet and must not contradict each other, unless either natural knowledge, on the one hand, or the causality of freedom required by practical reason in the world of sense, on the other, is to be impossible. Now the possibility of this agreement of two legislations entirely independent of one another can be conceived in no other way than by their common dependence on a higher legislation that underlies both but which is entirely inaccessible to us. If we were able to take its principle as a basis for a world view, then according to this principle one and the same effect would be cognized as fully necessary – an effect which appears to us in relation to the world of sense as *free* according to the moral law, and when attributed to the causality of reason, appears in nature as *contingent*. But since we are not able to do so, it plainly follows that as soon as we take into consideration a causality through freedom, we must assume that not all appearances in the world of sense are necessary according to natural laws alone, but rather that many of them are only contingent; and that accordingly we must not explain them all *from* the laws of nature, but rather some merely *according to* natural laws. *To explain something merely according to natural laws,* however, means to assume the causality of the matter of the effect to be outside of nature, but the causality of the form of the effect to be within nature. All appearances in the world of sense must be capable of explanation *according to* the laws of nature, for otherwise they could never become an object of knowledge.

Let us now apply these principles to that anticipated supernatural influence of God in the world of sense. God is to be thought of, in accordance with the postulates of reason, as that being who

determines nature in conformity with the moral law. In him, therefore, is the union of both legislations, and that principle on which
they mutually depend underlies his world view. For him, therefore,
nothing is natural and nothing supernatural, nothing is necessary
and nothing contingent, nothing is possible and nothing [109]
actual. Negatively we can assert this much for certain, obliged by
the laws of *our* thought; but if we wanted to determine the modality
of his understanding positively, we would become transcendent. So
there can be no question at all concerning how *God* could conceive
of a supernatural effect in the world of sense as possible and how he
could actually do it; but rather how *we* are able to conceive of an
appearance as effected by a supernatural causality of God.

   We are obliged by our reason to derive the entire system of
appearances, and ultimately the entire world of sense, from a
causality through freedom according to rational laws, and specifically
from God's causality. The entire world is for us a supernatural
effect of God. Thus it is surely conceivable that God has interwoven
the first natural cause of a certain appearance that was in accord
with one of his moral intentions into the plan of the whole at the
very beginning (for we may speak quite humanly, since here we are
not establishing objective truths but rather subjective possibilities of
thought). The objection that has been made against it – that it
means doing in a roundabout way what could be done directly – is
based on a gross anthropomorphism, as though God stood under
temporal conditions. In this case the appearance would be explained
wholly and perfectly from the laws of nature, right up to the supernatural origin of nature itself as a whole, if we could disregard the
latter in this context; and nevertheless it would also be viewed
simultaneously as being effected by the causality of a divine concept
of the moral purpose thereby to be achieved.

   Or we could assume, in the second place, that God has intervened
in the series of causes and effects, which has already begun and
continues according to natural laws, and has produced by immediate
causality of his moral concept a different effect than would have
resulted through the mere causality of natural beings according
to natural laws. Here again we have not determined at [110]
which link of the chain he should intervene, whether just at the one
immediately preceding the intended effect, or whether he could not
also do it perhaps at a link very far removed from it according to
time and intervening effects. If we assume the second case, we will

be able, if we know the laws of nature thoroughly, to explain the appearance under discussion correctly according to natural laws from the preceding appearance, and this one again from the preceding one, and so on perhaps to infinity, until finally, of course, we encounter an effect that we can no longer explain from natural laws but merely according to them. But granted that we would be able or willing to trace this series of natural causes only up to a certain point, it would then be quite possible that within these limits set by us that effect which is no longer to be explained naturally would not fall. But we would thereby still not be at all justified in concluding that the appearance under investigation could not in general be effected by a supernatural causality. Thus only in the first case would we encounter immediately from the experience a causality inexplicable from natural laws, which would make it possible theoretically for us to assume a supernatural causality for it.

But does God not will that the sensuous man, to whom he proves by this effect his identity as the author of the revelation, should acknowledge it as supernatural? It would not be proper to say that God wills us to draw that false conclusion, on which a *theoretical acknowledgment* of an appearance in nature as effected by a causality outside it is plainly based, according to the above discussion. But since it is not even supposed to ground conviction, which it cannot do, but simply attention, it is fully sufficient for this purpose, if for the time being, until we are capable of moral conviction, we accept it theoretically as only *possible* that it *may* have been effected by supernatural causality. And for this purpose (to conceive it as possible *theoretically*; for according to the discussion above, not even this much is required in order to find it *possible* morally) [111] nothing further is required than that *we* see no natural causes for this appearance. For it is conceived quite in accordance with reason: whenever I cannot explain an occurrence from natural causes, this comes about either because I do not know the natural laws according to which it is possible, or because according to such laws it is not possible in general.*

* If Christopher Columbus, instead of just extorting food from the inhabitants of Hispaniola by means of his supposed darkening of the moon, had used it with moral intentions as a divine attestation of a mission by him to them, I do not see how from a rational point of view they could have refused him their attention at first, since the success of this natural occurrence

Whom, then, does this 'we' include here? Plainly those, and only those, who are included in the plan to arouse attention. Let us take for granted, therefore, that after this purpose has been achieved and mankind is raised to the capability of a moral belief in the divinity of a revelation, it could be shown through increased insight into the laws of nature that certain appearances looked upon as supernatural, on which this revelation is based, are fully explicable from natural laws. From this alone, nothing at all could be inferred against the possible divinity of such a revelation, so long as this error is not based on arbitrary and willful deceit but merely on involuntary delusion, since an effect, especially when it is attributed to the original ground of all natural laws, can indeed be effected entirely naturally, and yet at the same time supernaturally, i.e., by the [112] causality of His freedom in accordance with the concept of a moral intention.

The result of what has been said here is that just as the dogmatic defender of the concept of revelation may not be permitted to infer a supernatural causality, and indeed the causality of God directly, from the inexplicability of a certain appearance from natural laws; so likewise the dogmatic opponent of this concept is not to be allowed to infer from the explicability of this same appearance from natural laws that it is possible neither by supernatural causality in general nor in particular by God's causality. The whole question may not be discussed dogmatically at all, according to theoretical principles, but rather it must be discussed morally, according to principles of practical reason, as follows sufficiently from everything that has been said up to now. How this would have to take place, however, will be shown in the course of this treatise

according to his definite prediction must have been utterly inexplicable for them according to natural laws. And if he had then founded on this attestation a religion fully in keeping with the principles of reason, not only would they by no means have lost something thereby, but they could even look upon it with full conviction as having immediate divine origin, until – through their own insight into natural laws and through the historical information that Columbus had known these laws just as well and that he thus had certainly not dealt honestly with them – they could no longer look upon this religion as divine *revelation*, to be sure, yet would remain bound to acknowledge it as divine *religion* because of its total agreement with the moral law.[29]

29 The editors of the *Gesamtausgabe* (p. 73 n.) note that Fichte has mistakenly placed the incident of the eclipse on Hispaniola though it in fact occurred while Columbus was on Jamaica on 29 February 1504.

§10

Criteria of the Divinity of a Revelation
According to Its Form[30]

In order to be able to convince ourselves rationally of the possibility that a given revelation is from God, we must have sure criteria of this divinity. Since the concept of a revelation is possible a priori, it is this concept itself to which we must hold a revelation given a posteriori; i.e., the criteria of its divinity must be derivable from this concept.

So far we have discussed the concept of revelation merely according to its form, insofar as this form must be religious,[31] in complete abstraction from the possible content of a revelation given *in concreto*. Up to now we have therefore had only to establish the criteria of the divinity of a revelation as far as its form is concerned. We can distinguish two different aspects, however, in the form of a revelation, i.e., in a simple proclamation of God as moral lawgiver through a supernatural appearance in the world of sense: namely, its *external* aspect, i.e., the circumstances under which, and [113] the means by which, this proclamation occurred; and then its *internal* aspect, i.e., the proclamation itself.

The concept of revelation a priori presupposes an empirically given moral need for it, without which reason was unable to conceive as morally possible a performance of the Deity, which was then superfluous and utterly pointless; and the empirical deduction of the conditions for the actuality of this concept developed this need. Thus it must be possible to show that this need was actually present at the time of origin of a revelation making claim to a divine origin, and that there was not already another existing religion, itself bearing all the criteria of divinity, among the same people for whom this revelation was determined, or that it could not easily have been communicated to them by natural means. *If this can be shown to be*

---

[30] *Gesamtausgabe*, pp. 74–7 (§8).
[31] The qualifying phrase 'insofar as this form must be religious' was added in the second edition.

the case, a revelation may be from God; if the opposite can be shown, it is certainly not from God.

It is necessary to establish this criterion expressly in order to check all fanaticism and all kinds of unqualified inspired persons at present or in the future. If a revelation is adulterated according to its content, it is the duty and right of every virtuous man to restore to it its original purity. But for this purpose no new divine authority is needed but merely an appeal to what is already available and the development of the truth out of our moral feeling. Even the possibility of two simultaneously existing divine revelations is not absolutely denied by this criterion, so long as the possessors of them are not in a position to communicate them to each other.

God is supposed to be the cause of the effects by which revelation takes place. Everything that is immoral, however, contradicts the concept of God. *Every revelation, therefore, that has proclaimed, maintained, or propagated itself by immoral means is certainly not from God.*

It is always immoral, whatever the intent may be, to deceive. Thus if an alleged divine emissary supports his authority by deceit, [114] God cannot have willed it. Moreover, a prophet actually supported by God does not need deceit. He is not carrying out his own intention but rather the intention of God and can therefore leave it utterly to God to what extent and how he will support this intention. However, someone might still say, the will of the divine emissary is free, and he may, perhaps with well-meaning intent, wish to do more than he is charged with, to attest the matter still further than it is already attested, and thereby be carried away into deceit; and then the cause of this deceit is not God but the man of whom he makes use.

We may not deny in general that God might make use of immoral or morally weak persons for the spreading of a revelation – for how could he avoid it, when no others are available? And where there is the greatest need of revelation there will certainly be no others. But he must also not permit them, at least in the execution of his commission, to use immoral means; he would have to prevent it by his omnipotence, if their free will should lead them to do so. For if the deceit were discovered – and any deceit may be – then two cases are possible. On the one hand, the aroused attention may disappear and its place be taken by irritation at seeing oneself deceived and distrust of everything that comes from these or similar sources – which contradicts the purpose intended by this arrangement in general. Or on the other hand, if the doctrine is already sufficiently authorized, deceit would thereby be authorized as well; everyone would consider himself to be fully sanctioned to do what a divine emissary is sanctioned to do – which contradicts morality and the concept of all religion.

The final purpose of every revelation is pure morality. This is possible only through freedom, and thus cannot be coerced. Not only morality, however, but also the attention to representations that aim at developing the feeling for it and at facilitating the [115] determination of the will in its conflict with inclination cannot be coerced; but coercion, on the contrary, is opposed to it. No divine religion, therefore, can have proclaimed or spread itself through coercion or persecution; for God can make use of no unsuitable means, nor even just allow the use of such means for intentions that are his own, because they would thereby be justified. Thus every revelation that has proclaimed and fortified itself by persecution is certainly not from God. *That revelation, however, which has made use of none but moral means for its proclamation and assertion may be from God.* These are the criteria of the divinity of a revelation with regard to its external form. We proceed to those of the internal form.

Every revelation is supposed to ground religion, and all religion is based on the concept of God as moral lawgiver. Thus a revelation that proclaims him to us as something else – one which wishes perhaps to acquaint us theoretically with his essence, or sets him up as a political lawgiver – is at all events not that which we are seeking: it is not revealed *religion*. *Every revelation, therefore, must proclaim God to us as moral lawgiver, and only one that has this as its purpose can we believe on moral grounds to be from God.*

Obedience towards the moral commands of God can be based only on reverence and on respect for his holiness, because only in this case is it purely moral. *Every revelation, therefore, that wishes to move us to obedience by other motives – e.g., by threatened punishments or promised rewards – cannot be from God,* for motives of this kind contradict pure morality.

It is certain, of course, and will be further amplified below that a revelation may either explicitly include the promises of the moral law as promises of God or guide us to search for them in our own

heart. But they must be established only as consequences [116]
and not as motives.*

* If it could be proved that a rational assent were possible to a revelation of
  God as political lawgiver – a possible assent together with which the
  possibility of the whole matter stands or falls (a proof that appears to be
  nearly impossible from what was said above in §5) – in that case, it would
  be clear that obedience to laws of that kind in such a revelation not only
  could be based on fear of punishment and hope of reward but would have
  to be, since the final purpose of political laws is mere legality, and it is
  most reliably effected by those incentives.

§11

Criteria of the Divinity of a Revelation With Regard to Its Possible Content (*materiæ revelationis*)[32]

The essential element of revelation in general is the proclamation of God as moral lawgiver through a supernatural effect in the world of sense. A revelation given *in concreto* may contain narratives of this effect, or of these effects, means, arrangements, circumstances, etc. Everything that has reference to such matters belongs to the external form of the revelation and stands under its criteria. Where the law itself, according to its content, may be set down by this proclamation of the lawgiver thereby remains totally undecided. The proclamation may refer us directly to our heart; or in addition it may also establish what our heart would tell us as God's special declaration, and then leave it to us ourselves to compare the latter with the former. The proclamation of God as lawgiver, composed in words, would say: God is moral lawgiver. And since we must compose it in words, we can also call it a *content*, namely, that *of the proclamation* in itself, the *meaning of the form of the revelation*. If besides this, however, still more is told to us, then the latter is the *content of the revelation*. We are able, to be sure, to conceive the former a priori; and if the need is given to us a posteriori, we can wish for and await it. But we can never realize it ourselves, but [117] rather the realization of this concept must occur by means of a fact in the world of sense. We can never know a priori, therefore, how and in what way the revelation will be given. The latter, namely, that a revelation in general may have a content, we cannot expect a priori, for it does not belong to the essence of revelation. But we can, on the other hand, know completely a priori what this content can be; and here, then, we stand immediately before the question: can we expect from a revelation teachings and explanations at which our reason, left to itself and guided by no supernatural aid, would never have arrived – not merely under the contingent conditions under which our reason was and is, but according to its nature in general? And we may proceed to the answer all the more calmly,

[32] *Gesamtausgabe*, pp. 77–89 (§9).

since, in case we must answer in the negative (according to the deduction above, in which we were concerned really with the form of the revelation) we have no longer to fear the objection that revelation would be superfluous in general if it were able to teach us nothing new.

These teachings to be created solely from supernatural sources could have as their object either the extension of our theoretical knowledge of the supersensuous or the closer determination of our duties. So can we expect extension of our theoretical knowledge from a revelation? The answer to this question is based on the following two questions: is such an extension *morally* possible, i.e., is it not contrary to pure morality? And then: is it *physically* possible; does it not perhaps contradict the nature of things? And finally: does it not perhaps contradict the concept of revelation, and consequently itself?

Is it morally possible? The ideas of the supersensuous, which are realized by practical reason, are *freedom*, *God*, and *immortality*. It is immediate *fact* that in respect to our higher faculty of [118] desire we are free, i.e., that we have a higher faculty of desire independent of natural laws. By means of our moral determination to will the final purpose of the moral law, we are directly enjoined to believe that which we need in respect to the concept of God for the moral determination of our will: that there *is* a God, and that he is the *Only Holy*, the *Only Just*, the *Omnipotent*, and the *Omniscient One*, the supreme lawgiver and judge of all rational beings. That we must be *immortal* follows immediately from the requirement that our finite natures realize the highest good, a demand which they as such are not capable of satisfying, but *ought* to become more and more capable of doing, and must therefore be *able* to do. What more do we still want to know about these ideas? Do we want to discover the connection of the natural law and the one for freedom in the supersensuous substratum of nature? Unless at the same time we receive the power to govern the laws of nature through our freedom, it cannot have the slightest practical usefulness for us. But if we do receive it, we cease to be finite beings and become gods. Do we want to have a *definite* concept of God, to know his essence as it *is in itself*? Not only will this not further pure morality, but it will hinder it. An infinite being that we know, that hovers in his entire majesty before our eyes, will drive and push us forcefully to fulfill his commands; freedom will be abolished;

sensuous inclination will fall silent forever; we will lose all the profit and all the practice, strengthening, and joy through the struggle, and from free beings with limited knowledge will have become moral machines with extended knowledge. Do we want, finally, even now to penetrate all the determinations of our future existence? Partly, it will rob us of all the sensations of Happiness that the gradual improvement of our condition can give us. We will squander all at once what is destined for us for an eternal existence. And partly, the rewards hovering before us will again determine us too powerfully and take from us freedom, profit, and self-respect. All such knowledge will not increase, but [119] rather decrease, our morality; and God cannot will this. It is, therefore, morally impossible. And is it physically possible? Does it not utterly conflict with the laws of nature, i.e., of *our* nature, to which these teachings are supposed to be given? Anything a revelation might possibly teach us about the supersensuous must be adapted to our faculty of cognition; its teachings must stand under the laws of our thought. These laws are the categories, without which no definite representation is possible for us. If its teachings were not so adapted, the whole instruction would be lost for us; it would be utterly incomprehensible and inconceivable to us, and we would be no better off than if we did not have it. If the teachings were so adapted, the supersensuous objects would be drawn down into the sensuous world; the supernatural would be made into a part of nature. I am not investigating here whether such an objectification for the senses, given as objectively valid, does not contradict practical reason – which will become clear further on. It is clear at once, however, that we would thereby receive a knowledge of something supersensuous that would not be supersensuous, and that we would thus not achieve our purpose of being introduced into the world of the spirits but rather would lose even that correct insight into it which is possible for us from the standpoint of practical reason. Finally, does not such an expectation indeed contradict the nature of revelation?* Teachings of this kind directed to our reason as

---

* I ask everyone to whom the assertion to be proved here still seems offensive to pay particular attention to what follows from here on. *Either* the entire critique of revelation must be invalidated and the possibility of an a posteriori theoretical conviction of the divinity of a given revelation confirmed (about which one has to rely on §5); *or* one must grant the proposition unconditionally that a revelation cannot extend our supersensuous knowledge. [Note added in the second edition.]

determined by the moral law could not even be considered in order to test whether or not they agree with it, since they would not [120] be based on *these principles* at all (for if they were based on them, our reason, left to itself, would have to have been able to arrive at them without any alien assistance). For this reason, faith in their truth could be based on nothing except, perhaps, the divine *authority* to which a revelation appeals. But then no other ground of faith occurs for this divine authority itself except the *conformity to reason* (the agreement, not with the sophistical, but with the morally believing reason) of the doctrines that are based on it. Hence, *this divine authority cannot itself be the ground for attesting something that is supposed to attest it in the first place.*

If another way than this one for arriving at the rational acknowledgment of the divinity of a revelation were conceivable – if, for example, miracle or prophecy, i.e., if in general the inexplicability of an occurrence from natural causes could justify us in ascribing its origin to the direct causality of God (an inference which, however, as is shown above, would plainly be false) – then it could be conceived how our conviction, grounded thereby, of the divinity of a given revelation in general could ground our faith in each of its individual teachings. But since this faith in the divinity of a revelation in general is possible only through faith in each of its individual declarations, no revelation as such can certify the truth of any assertion which cannot do the same for itself. Thus from a rational point of view a faith is not possible in any teaching that is possible only through revelation; and any requirement of this kind would contradict the possibility of the assent which takes place in a revelation, and hence the concept of revelation in itself. Therefore, what the critique thwarted for us from the side of theoretical reason left to itself, a transition into the supersensuous world, we also must not expect from revelation. Rather, we must give up this hope of a definite knowledge of it for our present nature totally, for [121] ever, and from every source.*

---

* In order to reject rash consequences and illicit applications, we note explicitly once again that only propositions proclaimed as *objectively* valid are under discussion here, and that a great deal that appears to be extending our knowledge of the supersensuous may be the presentation in sensuous form of immediate rational postulates, or of ones arising through their application to certain experiences. Hence, if this is demonstrably the case, it would not be excluded by this criterion. The proof of it, however, does not belong here but rather in the applied critique of a particular revelation.

Or, can we expect from a revelation, perhaps, practical maxims, moral precepts which we were unable also to derive for ourselves from the principle of all morality, out of and by means of our reason? The moral law in us is the voice of pure reason, of reason *in abstracto*. Not only can reason not contradict itself, but it also cannot make different statements in different subjects, because its command is the purest unity and thus difference would at the same time be contradiction. Reason speaks to *us* as it speaks to all rational beings, as it speaks to God himself. He can give us, therefore, neither another principle nor precepts for special cases which would be based on another principle, for he himself is determined by no other principle. The particular rule that arises through application of the principle to a particular case is certainly different depending on the situations that the subject can get into according to its nature;* but they all must be derivable by one and the same reason, from one and the same reason. It is another matter to ask whether subjects determined empirically and given *in concreto* will derive the rule in particular cases with equal correctness and facility, and whether in doing so they may not need alien assistance to guide them in their own derivation – but not to do it for them and then give them [122] the result as correct on its authority, for even if the rule were correctly derived, this would nevertheless ground only legality and not morality. But for this purpose no revelation is needed, but rather every wiser person can and should do it for the one less wise.

It is therefore possible neither morally nor theoretically for a revelation to give us teachings at which our reason could not and should not have arrived without it. *And no revelation can require faith for teachings of this sort*; for it would not happen that the divine origin of a revelation would be completely denied solely for this reason, since alleged teachings of this kind, although they cannot be derived from the law of practical reason, nevertheless do not necessarily have to contradict it.

But what can it then contain if it is to contain nothing unfamiliar to us? Doubtless precisely that to which practical reason leads us a priori: a moral law and its postulates.

As far as the morality possible through a revelation is concerned,

---

* So this is certainly a correct rule: never make a decision in the heat of emotion. But even this rule, as empirically conditioned, cannot have universal application to men, for it is quite possible, and should be possible, to make oneself totally free of all surging emotions.

the distinction was already made above that the same revelation may either refer us directly to the law of reason within us as God's law, or it may establish the principle of reason, in itself as well as in application to possible cases, under divine authority.

If the former happens, such a revelation contains no morality, but rather our own reason contains its morality. Thus it is only the second case that comes under investigation here. The revelation establishes as laws of God partly the principle of all morality put into words, and partly particular maxims arising through its application to empirically conditioned cases. It is immediately clear that the principle of morality would have to be stated correctly, i.e., it would have to be fully in accord with that of the moral law within us, and that a religion *whose moral principle contradicts this could not be from God*; just as the warrant for proclaiming this principle as God's law already belongs to the form of a revelation and is [123] deduced simultaneously with it. With respect to the particular moral precepts, however, the question arises: is a revelation supposed to derive each of these particular rules from the moral principle proclaimed as divine law, or may it ground them simply, without further proof, on divine authority?

If the divine authority to command us is based just on his holiness alone, which the very form of every religion that is supposed to be divine requires, then respect for his command *because* it is his command is none other than respect for the moral law itself, even in particular cases. Consequently, a revelation may establish commandments of this kind simply as God's commands without further deduction from the principle. It is another question, however, whether it would not have to be possible at least subsequently to deduce each of these particular precepts of a revealed morality correctly from the principle, and whether every revelation would not in the end have to refer us to this principle after all.

We can convince ourselves of the possibility of the divine origin of a revelation, in general as well as each particular part of its content, only through its complete agreement with practical reason. This conviction, however, in the case of a particular moral maxim, is possible only by its derivation from the principle of all morality. It therefore follows directly that every maxim established as *moral* in a divine revelation would have to be derivable from this principle. Now a maxim that cannot be *derived* from it still does not thereby become false, but rather it follows only that it does not belong in the

field of morality; but it may perhaps belong in the realm of theory –
it may be political, technico-practical,[33] or the like. Take, for
example, that saying: Shall we do evil that good may come of it?
By no means![34] This is a general moral command, because it can be
deduced from the principle of all morality, and the opposite would
contradict it. On the other hand, those maxims, If anyone would
sue you for your coat, let him have your cloak as well,[35] etc., are not
moral precepts but rules of policy valid only in particular [124]
cases, which as such have validity only so long as they do not come
into collision with a moral precept, because everything must be
subordinated to these precepts. If a revelation, then, contains rules
of the latter kind, it still by no means follows that the whole revelation is therefore not divine, and just as little that those rules are
false (that depends on further proofs from the principles under
which they stand), but only that these rules do not belong to the
content of a revealed religion as such but that their worth must
derive from somewhere else. A revelation, however, which contains
maxims that contradict the principle of all morality – which
authorize, for example, pious or impious deceit, intolerance of those
who think differently, the spirit of persecution; which in general
authorize means other than teaching for spreading the truth – is
certainly not from God, for the will of God is in accord with the
moral law, and whatever contradicts it he can neither will nor can
he permit someone to proclaim as his will who otherwise acts at his
command.

Secondly, it is impossible a priori, by means of a finite understanding, to foresee all the particular cases in which moral laws
arise, or, by means of an infinite understanding that does foresee
them, to communicate them to finite beings; consequently, no revelation can contain all the possible particular rules of morality. For
this reason, a revelation must still refer us finally either to the moral
law within us or to a universal principle thereof, established by the
revelation as divine, which is identical with it. This belongs to the
very form, and a revelation that does not do it is not in agreement

---

[33] Reading *technisch-praktisch* instead of *technisch, praktisch* as actually
printed in the second edition. The first edition originally read *technisch,
practisch*, but the list of errata published subsequently corrected it to read
technisch-praktisch. Presumably, the original error was inadvertently carried over to the second edition.
[34] Cf. Rom. 3.8; 6.1–2.
[35] Cf. Matt. 5.40.

with its own concept and is not a revelation. There is no a priori law of reason available to determine whether it wills to do the former, the latter, or both.

The universal criterion of the divinity of a religion with respect to its moral content is, therefore, the following: *only that revelation can be from God which establishes a principle of morality that agrees with the principle of practical reason and only such* [125] *moral maxims as can be derived therefrom.*

The second part of the possible content of a religion are those propositions which as postulates of reason are certain, and which presuppose the possibility of the final purpose of the moral law in sensuously conditionable beings – which, therefore, are given simultaneously by the determination of our will, and by which in return the determination of our will is reciprocally facilitated. This part of the content of a religion is called *dogmatics*, and it can continue to be called by this name if in so doing one looks only to its matter and not to the manner of proof and does not believe oneself to be justified by this term in *dogmatizing*, i.e., in presenting these propositions as objectively valid. It has already been proved above that a revelation could teach us nothing further about these propositions than what follows from the principles of pure reason. So there remains to be discussed here only the question: on what can a revelation ground our faith in these truths? According to the discussions above, the following two cases are still possible: either the revelation derives them from the moral law within us, which it establishes as God's law, and thereby gives them to us only indirectly[36] as God's assurances; or it established them directly as resolutions of the Deity, either simply as such or as resolutions of his being, determined by the moral law, yet without expressly deriving them from this law. The first way of founding our faith is wholly in accord with the procedure of rational and natural religion, and its legitimacy is hence beyond doubt. With the second way the following two questions arise: does it not impair our freedom, and thus our morality, if we view the merely postulated promises of the moral law as promises of an infinite being? And: must not all these assurances be derivable from the final purpose of the moral law, at least subsequently? As for the first question, it is clear at once that if a revelation has presented God to us simply as the Only Holy

---

[36] Reading *mittelbar* with the first edition; the second edition and the *Sämmtliche Werke* have *unmittelbar*, an apparent misprint.

One, as the strictest reproduction of the moral law (as every [126] revelation should do), then all belief in God is belief in the moral law presented *in concreto*. As far as the second question is concerned, however, if a certain doctrine cannot be derived from the final purpose of the moral law, there are again two cases possible: either it is *merely not derivable*, or it *contradicts* it.

If certain dogmatic assertions contradict the final purpose of the moral law, they contradict the concept of God and the concept of all religion; *and a revelation that contains assertions of this kind cannot be from God.* Not only can God not justify assertions of this kind, but he cannot even allow them in connection with a purpose that is his own, because they contradict his purpose. But if some of them are simply not derivable from it without directly contradicting it,[37] it is still not to be inferred that the entire revelation could not be from God; for God avails himself of the service of men who err, who can even invent a chimera for themselves in order to place it, perhaps with well-meaning intent, alongside divine teachings and to promote still more good according to their opinion. And it is not proper for him to limit their freedom unless they want to make use of it in a way directly opposed to his purpose. But it follows for certain *that everything of this kind is not a constituent of a divine revelation but rather a human supplement,* of which we have to take no further notice except insofar as its value becomes clear from other grounds. Propositions of this kind, since they are wholly incapable of moral intention, are able generally to promise only theoretical disclosures; and when they talk about supernatural things, they will usually be incapable of conception because they cannot stand under the conditions of the categories. If they did stand under these conditions as objective assertions, not only would they not be derivable but they would even contradict the moral law, as will be demonstrated in the following chapter.

Finally, a revelation may put forward certain means for encouraging and furthering virtue, which may be combined with a greater or lesser degree of ceremony, and may be for use in society or [127] by oneself alone. Since all religion presents God only as moral lawgiver, everything that is not a commandment of the moral law within us is likewise not his commandment, and there is no means for pleasing him except by observing this law. The means for furthering virtue must not, therefore, turn into virtue itself; these

[37] Reading *ihm* instead of *ihnen*, an apparent error.

recommendations of virtue must not turn into *commandments* that impose a duty on us; it must not be left ambiguous whether one might earn the approval of the Deity for oneself also by the use of these means, or perhaps *only thereby*, but rather their relationship to the actual moral law must be precisely defined.

When a wise being wills the end, he also wills the means, one might say. But he wills them only insofar as they really are means and becomes means, and – since these are means to be applied in the world of sense, and we thus enter here into the area of the concept of nature – he can will them only insofar as they lie in our power. It is very true, for example, and anyone who prays discovers it, that prayer – whether it be the worshipping contemplation of God, or petition, or thanksgiving – effectively silences our sensibility and mightily exalts our heart to the feeling and love of our duties. But how can we oblige the cold man who is capable of no enthusiasm – and it is quite possible that there may be such – to inspire his contemplation and to exalt it to worship? How can we compel him to enliven ideas of reason by presenting them with the help of the imagination, if subjective causes have deprived him of this ability, since it is an empirical determination? How can we compel him to feel any need so strongly, to long for it so fervently, that he would forget himself in order to communicate this need to a supernatural being, when by thinking coolly he recognizes that He knows it without him and that He will give it without him, if he earns it and must have it and his need is not imaginary?

Aids such as these, therefore, are only to be presented as [128] what they are, and are not to be equated with the actions commanded unconditionally by the moral law. They are not simply to be commanded but are merely to be recommended to the one whose need drives him to them. They are less a command than a permission. *Every revelation that equates them with moral laws is certainly not from God*, for it contradicts the moral law to put anything else in the same rank with its requirements.

But what effects on our moral nature may a revelation promise from such means – merely natural ones, or supernatural ones, i.e., ones which according to the laws of nature are not connected necessarily with them as effects with their causes, but rather are effected by a supernatural cause external to us whenever an occasion for using them arises? Let us for a moment assume the latter, namely, that our will is determined *in accord with the moral law* by a supernatural cause external to us. But then no determination that does not occur by and with freedom is in accord with the moral law; consequently, this assumption contradicts itself, and any action resulting from such a determination would not be moral. It could have, consequently, neither the slightest merit nor in any way become for us a source of respect and Happiness. We would in this case be machines and not moral beings, and an action produced thereby would simply be nil in the series of our moral actions.

But even if one should have to admit this, as one must, one could still say further: when an occasion for using those means arises, such a determination ought to be produced in us, not in order to raise *our* morality, which of course would not be possible, but in order, rather, by means of the effect that is produced in us supernaturally to produce a series in the world of sense which would become the means for determining *other* moral beings according to the laws of nature, and whereby *we* would admittedly be mere machines. The fact that God would make use of us rather than others for this purpose, however, would depend on the condition for the use of that means.

Now without investigating just what value it might have [129] for us whether *we* are used as machines or whether other machines are used for furthering the good – even in this regard, a revelation cannot make promises of this kind; for if everyone fulfilled its condition and everyone thereby brought about an alien, supernatural causality in himself, not only would all laws of nature outside us be thereby suspended but also all morality within us. We cannot simply deny, however, that effects of this kind might in particular cases have been in the plan of the Deity without denying the principle of revelation in general. Neither can we deny that some of these effects may have been bound to conditions on the part of the instruments, because we cannot know that. But whenever narratives of such effects or precepts and promises regarding them are found in a revelation, they belong to the external form of the revelation and not to its universal content. Determination by supernatural causes external to us suspends morality; *every religion, therefore, that promises determinations of this kind under any condition contradicts the moral law and is therefore certainly not from God.*

There is nothing left, therefore, for revelation to promise from such means except natural effects. As soon as we speak of means for furthering virtue, we are in the province of the concept of nature. The means is within sensuous nature;[38] what is to be determined thereby is the sensuous nature within us. Our ignoble inclinations are to be weakened and suppressed; our nobler ones are to be strengthened and increased. The moral determination of the will is not supposed to occur thereby but only to be facilitated. Therefore, everything must necessarily be connected as cause and effect, and this connection must be clearly perceivable.

But it is not hereby asserted that revelation might be claimed to demonstrate this connection. The purpose of revelation is practical, but such a deduction is theoretical and can be left accordingly [130] to the individual reflection of each person. Revelation can be satisfied to establish these means merely as recommended by God. But it must be possible subsequently to show this connection; for God, who knows our sensuous nature, can commend to it no means for betterment which are not in accord with its own laws. Every revelation, therefore, which proposes means for furthering virtue, concerning which it cannot be shown how they can contribute naturally thereto, is not – at least *insofar as it does this* – from God.

We may here append this limitation: provided that such means are not made into duties, provided that supernatural effects are not promised by them, then their recommendation is not contradictory to morality, but it is merely empty and useless.*

---

* It does not at all follow, however, that because a certain means is of no use to a subject, or even to the majority, it could therefore have no uses for anyone. And it seems to me that people have gone too far in recent times in rejecting many ascetic practices out of hatred for the abuse formerly promoted by them. Everyone who has worked on himself knows that it is good and useful in general to suppress his sensibility occasionally even where no explicit law speaks, merely in order to weaken it and to become ever freer.

38 The first edition includes the following parenthesis at this point: '. . . (also prayer, although its origin is supersensuous) . . .'

§12

Criteria of the Divinity of a Revelation
With Regard to
the Possible Presentation of This Content[39]

Since revelation in general exists according to its very form for the
need of sensibility, it is very probable that it would condescend to it
also in its presentation if it should be shown that sensibility has
special needs in this connection. Yet this presentation is so far from
being the essential and characteristic feature of a revelation that, as
was shown above, we cannot even require a priori that it have a
content or do anything more in general than proclaim God to be
the author of the moral law.

Sensibility, because of the opposition of inclination, is [131]
in general only too ready to take the fulfillment of the moral law to
be impossible and not to acknowledge the commandment as having
been given for *it*. Now to be sure, revelation gives this law explicitly
to sensibility; yet the voice of duty still speaks in the sensuous man
only softly, weakened by the crying of desire and muted by the
false concepts it supplies in abundance, whenever it is supposed to
speak about his own actions – whenever it is *commanding*, in the
truest sense. But even the most grossly sensuous person hears it
whenever the question concerns the judgment of an action in which
his inclination is in no way involved. And if only he learns in this
way to distinguish the voice of duty in himself, if only in this way
it is drawn out of its indolence and he becomes more familiar and
intimate with it, he will at last begin also to hate in *himself* what he
abhors in others and to wish for himself what he demands of others.

The absurdity of wanting to have everything around oneself be
just and only to be unjust oneself is too striking for any person to
want to admit it to himself. If only one might bring him to the point
that in the event he is unjust he would have to admit it to himself!
How can this purpose be achieved? By setting up moral examples.
Revelation can thus clothe its morality in narratives, and it only
meets the need of man all the better when it does so. It can set up unjust actions to be despised and just ones, especially those accomplished

[39] *Gesamtausgabe*, pp. 89–96 (§10).

139

with great sacrifices and efforts, to be admired and imitated. No question can arise concerning the warrant of a revelation to expound its moral doctrine in this way. And it follows from the purpose of revelation that the actions established by it as exemplary must be purely moral; that it must not praise ambiguous, or even plainly bad, actions as good and commend people as examples who have performed such actions. *Every revelation that does this contradicts the moral law and the concept of God and can* [132] *consequently not be of divine origin.*

A revelation has to present the ideas of reason: freedom, God, immortality.

Each person's self-consciousness teaches him directly that man is free; and the less he has adulterated his natural feeling by sophistical reasoning, the less he doubts it. The possibility of all religion and all revelation presupposes freedom. The presentation of this idea for the sensuously conditioned reason is therefore not the business of a revelation. And no revelation has to do with dissolving the dialectical pseudo-arguments against this idea; it does not subtilize but command, and is directed not to sophistical subjects but to sensuous ones.

But the idea of God is against it all the more. Everyone who is a human being, if he wants to conceive of God, is forced to conceive of him under the conditions of pure sensibility, time and space. We may be ever so convinced, and able to prove so very rigorously, that these conditions do not suit him; yet this error takes us by surprise while we are still censuring it. We want to think of God as present to us now, and we cannot avoid thinking of him as being in the place where we are. We want to think of God now as the foreseer of our future fortunes, of our free resolutions, and we think of him as being in the time in which he now is, looking into a time in which he is not yet. To such representations the presentation of a religion must adapt itself; for it speaks with human beings and can speak no language but that of human beings.

But empirical sensibility is in need of still more. The inner sense, the empirical self-consciousness, stands under the condition that it must take in a manifold gradually and by degrees and add them to one another, that it can take in nothing that is not distinguished from the antecedent, and that it can therefore perceive only changes. Its world is a ceaseless chain of modifications. It wants to think also of God's self-consciousness under this condition.

The inner sense now needs, for example, a witness to the purity of its attitudes in connection with a certain resolution. 'God [133] has *perceived*,' so it thinks to itself, 'what went on in my soul.' It is now ashamed of an immoral action; its conscience reminds it of the holiness of the lawgiver. 'He has *discovered* it,' it thinks, 'he has discovered the entire corruption that is exhibited therein. But he perceives also the remorse that I now feel about it,' it continues. It now resolves really strongly to work attentively henceforth on its sanctification. It feels that it lacks the powers to do so. It wrestles with itself; and being too weak in battle, it looks around for alien assistance and prays to God. 'At my fervent, persistent supplication, God will *decide* to assist me,' it thinks – and thinks of God in all these cases as modifiable by it. It conceives of emotions and passions in God so that he can participate in its own emotions and passions: sympathy, pity, mercy, love, pleasure, etc.

The highest or lowest level of sensibility, which places everything under the empirical conditions of external sense, demands still more. It wants a corporeal God, who *sees* its actions, in the truest sense, *hears* its words, with whom it might speak as one friend with another. Whether a revelation might be able to condescend to these needs is not a question; whether it is permitted to do so, however, and to what extent it is permitted, is what a critique of revelation must answer.

The purpose of all these teachings is none other than the furthering of pure morality and its presentation in sensuous form, especially furthering pure morality in the sensuous man. Only insofar as this objectification for the senses agrees with this purpose can the revelation be divine; but if it contradicts it, it is certainly not divine.

The sensuous objectification of the concept of God may contradict God's moral attributes in two different ways: in part, namely, *directly*, if God is presented with passions that are directly opposed to the moral law – if, for example, wrath and vengeance are ascribed to him on account of willfulness, partiality, or prejudice, which are based on something other than the morality of the objects [134] of these passions. Such a God would not be a model for our imitation and a being for whom we could have respect but rather an object of an anxious, despair-producing fear. However, this contradicts the very form of all revelation, which demands a *holy* God as lawgiver. But it would not contradict the moral concept of God at all, if, for

example, spirited indignation over the immoral behavior of finite
beings were ascribed to him; for that is merely sensuous presentation of a necessary effect of God's holiness, which we are quite
incapable of cognizing as it is in itself in God. And even if this
indignation were called wrath in a language that had no definite
words for the finer modifications of the emotions, even this does not
contradict the concept of God understood in the spirit of the people
speaking this language. *Every* sensuous presentation of God would
contradict morality *indirectly* if it were represented as *objectively
valid* and not as mere condescension to our *subjective need*. For I
can draw inferences from anything that is true of the object in itself
and thereby define it further. If we derive inferences as objectively
valid from any sensuous condition of God, however, we get more
deeply entangled with every step in contradictions with his moral
attributes. If God actually sees and hears, for example, he must also
partake of enjoyment by means of these senses; then it is quite possible for us to give him sensuous enjoyment, and the odor of burnt
offerings and oblations can actually please him;* and we thus [135]
have other means for becoming pleasing to him than morality. If
we are really able to determine God by our sensations, to move him
to sympathy, pity, or joy, then he is not the Unchangeable, the Only
Sufficient, the Only Holy One, and he is still determinable by something other than the moral law. Indeed, we can even hope by
whining and contrition to move him to deal with us otherwise than
the degree of our morality may have earned. All these sensuous
presentations of divine attributes must therefore not be proclaimed
as objectively valid. It must not be left ambiguous whether God is
thus constituted *in himself*, or whether he will permit us to think
of him thus only for the benefit of our sensuous need.

Beyond these conditions, however, we cannot prescribe laws a
priori for a revelation governing how far it may go in rendering the
concept of God in sensuous form; rather, it depends entirely on the

---

* The representations of the prophets against this error testify to the fact
that the Jews of ancient times actually made this inference; the ridiculously
childish representations of God contained in their Talmud prove that they
are no smarter in more recent times – whether through their own fault or
that of their religion remains unexamined here.
  But wherever does the delusion come from among many Christians of
medieval and more recent times that certain invocations – e.g., 'Kyrie
eleison,' 'Father of Our Lord Jesus Christ,' etc. – please him more than
others?

empirically-given need of the age for which it is first determined. For example, some revelation, in order on the one hand to meet all the needs of the grossest sensibility and on the other hand to ensure the concept of God its full purity, might present us with some thoroughly sensuously conditioned being as a reproduction of God's moral attributes insofar as they relate to human beings – a personified practical reason (λόγος), as it were, as a God of human beings. That would still be no reason at all to deny the divine origin of such a revelation in general or even just of this presentation of it, so long as this being were so represented that it could correspond to that intention, and so long as this substitution were not asserted to be objectively valid but were merely represented as condescension to sensibility, which might need it,* and – as follows necessarily from this – everyone were left the full option to make use of this representation or not, according as he might find it morally useful [136] for himself. *Only such a revelation, therefore, can be of divine origin as offers an anthropomorphic God not as objectively, but only as subjectively, valid.*

The concept of the immortality of the soul is based on an abstraction which sensibility, especially the lowest degree of sensibility, does not make. Everyone is sure of his personhood immediately through his self-consciousness. He cannot be robbed by any sophistry of the 'I am...an autonomous being.' But he does not differentiate, and is incapable of differentiating, which of these determinations of this 'I,' his ego [*dieses seines Ich*], are pure or empirical; which ones are given for and by the inner or outer sense, or which ones are given by pure reason; which are essential, and which only contingent and dependent only on his present situation. Perhaps he will never arrive at the concept of a soul as a pure spirit; and even if one gives it to him, one will often give him nothing but a word that is without meaning for him. He is thus able to think of the endurance of his ego in no other way than in the form of its endurance with all of its present determinations. If a revelation wishes to condescend to this weakness – and it will almost have to in order to become understandable – it will clothe that idea for him in the only form in which he is capable of conceiving it, in the form of the endurance of everything that he presently includes in his ego – and, since he plainly foresees the future destruction of one part of

* Jesus did not say, He who has seen me has seen the Father, until Philip asked him to *show* him the Father [cf. John 14.8–9].

it, in the form of resurrection,* and the producing of complete congruency between morality and Happiness in the image [137] of a universal trial and judgment day and a distribution of punishments and rewards. But it may not establish these images as objective truths.[40]

Only such a revelation can be divine, therefore, which offers a presentation in sensuous form of our immortality and of God's moral judgment of finite beings, not as objectively valid, but only subjectively (that is, not for human beings in general, but only for those sensuous human beings who need such a presentation). If it does the former, it is still not therefore to be denied the possibility of a divine origin in general; for such an assertion does not *contradict* morality, it is merely *not to be derived* from its principles. *But it is not, at least in regard to this assertion, divine.*   [139]

Whether a revelation attributes objective or merely subjective validity to its representations of ideas of pure reason in sensuous form, is to be observed from whether or not it builds upon these inferences – unless the revelation draws attention to it explicitly, which is still to be desired in order to avoid all possible misunderstanding. If it does build upon them, it is obvious that it attributes objective validity to them.

---

* It becomes clear that Jesus, for example, thought of immortality whenever he spoke of resurrection and that both concepts were at that time considered as fully equivalent, beyond his speeches in John on this subject, where he expounds the uninterrupted endurance of his adherents in a few sayings quite purely without the image of the resurrection, yet without discussing the difference between soul and body, and the possible objection of bodily death. It quite plainly becomes clear, among other passages, from that proof κατ' ἄνθρωπον against the Sadducees [cf. Matt. 22.23–33; Mark 12.18–27; Luke 20.27–40]. The saying of God referred to, granting everything else as correct, was able to prove nothing more than the [137] enduring existence of Abraham, Isaac, and Jacob in the time of Moses but no real resurrection of the flesh. That the Sadducees also understood it this way and denied not merely the bodily resurrection but immortality in general follows from the fact that they were satisfied with this proof of Jesus.

The contradictions that result from too crude a representation of this doctrine already forced Paul to define it somewhat more closely [cf. 1 Cor. 15].

[40] A lengthy passage at this point in the first edition, which was omitted in the second, is translated in the Appendix, pp. 177–8 below. I. H. Fichte retains it in the *Sämmtliche Werke* as a 'supplement from the first edition.'

Finally, since empirical sensibility changes according to its particular modifications among different peoples and in different ages, and should diminish more and more under the discipline of a good revelation, it is a criterion – not, of course, of the divinity of a revelation, but still of its possible determination for many peoples and times – whenever the bodies in which the spirit is clothed are not too firm and too durable, but rather are lightly sketched and adaptable without difficulty to the spirit of different peoples and times.

The very same thing holds good for the means of encouraging and furthering morality which a revelation recommends. Under the guidance of a wise revelation that is in wise hands, the former and latter ought more and more to give up their admixture of crude sensibility, because this ought to become more and more dispensable.

Systematic Order of These Criteria[41]

The criteria now established are conditions of the possibility of applying our a priori concept of a revelation to a given appearance in the world of sense and of judging whether it is a revelation – that is, not conditions of the application of the concept in general, for we will speak of these only in the following chapter, but rather conditions of its application to definite, given experience. In order to be sure that we have exhausted all these conditions and that there are no more besides the ones cited (for if, on the contrary, we had established some that were not, it would necessarily have [140] followed from the fact that we would not have been able to derive them from the concept of revelation), we must look around for a guide in discovering all determinations of this concept. And such a guide for all possible concepts is the table of the categories.[42]

The concept of a revelation, namely, is a concept of an appearance in the world of sense which, according to *quality*, is supposed to be effected directly by divine causality. It is hence a criterion of an appearance corresponding to this concept that it not be effected by any means that contradict the concept of a divine causality; and since we have only a moral concept of God, these include all immoral means. This appearance should be valid for all sensuous human beings who need it, according to *subjective quantity* (for *objective* quantity furnishes no real criterion; rather, on it is based merely the recollection that several revelations are not impossible among distant peoples at the same time). It is hence a condition of every revelation given *in concreto* that people with such a need can actually be pointed out.

These are the criteria of a revelation according to its external form, which follow from the mathematical determinations of its concept – that is, what had to be the case according to the nature of the subject matter.

This appearance, according to *relation*, is related in its concept to

[41] *Gesamtausgabe*, pp. 97–8 (§11).
[42] Cf. Kant, *Critique of Pure Reason*, p. 113 (B 106).

a purpose, namely, that of furthering pure morality. Consequently, a revelation given *in concreto* must demonstrably intend this purpose – but not achieve it necessarily, which would contradict the very concept of moral, i.e., free, beings, in whom alone morality can be produced. The furthering of this purpose in sensuous human beings, however, is possible in no other way than through the proclamation of God as moral lawgiver; and obedience to this lawgiver is moral only when it is based on the representation of his holiness. This proclamation, as well as the purity of the established motive of the obedience demanded, is hence a criterion of [141] every revelation.

Finally, as far as *modality* is concerned, a revelation was assumed in its concept merely to be possible, from which no condition of the application of this concept to an appearance given *in concreto* can follow, i.e., no criterion of a revelation, since it adds nothing to the concept in itself but only expresses the relation of its object to our understanding. What follows from this for the possibility of applying it in general, however, we will see in the following chapter.

These, then, are the criteria of a revelation according to its form; and since the essence of revelation consists precisely in the particular form of a matter already at hand a priori, they are the only criteria essential to it. And besides the ones established, no more are possible, because there are no more determinations in its concept.

The matter of a revelation is already present a priori through pure practical reason and stands, properly speaking, under precisely the same critique as practical reason itself. Hence, its only criterion, insofar as it is regarded as the matter of a revelation, according to the content as well as the presentation which modifies it, is that it agree fully with the testimony of practical reason: according to quality, that it declare just that; according to quantity, that it not pretend to want to declare more (for it is impossible that less should be declared in a revelation, since it has to establish a principle in which everything that can become the content of a religion must be contained, though perhaps undeveloped); according to relation, as something to be derived and subordinated to the only moral principle; and according to modality, as universally valid, not objectively, but only subjectively.

According to what has now been said, it would be easy to sketch a table of all criteria of every possible revelation following the order of the categories.

The Possibility of Receiving a Given Appearance As Divine Revelation[43]

Up to now nothing more has really been settled than the complete conceivability of a revelation in general, i.e., that the concept of such a revelation does not contradict itself. And since an appearance in the world of sense is postulated in this concept, the conditions had to be stipulated under which this concept is applicable to an appearance. These conditions were the determinations of the concept to be applied, which were discovered by an analysis.

What has not yet occurred, however – indeed, no preparations have even been made for it – is to assure this concept a reality *external to us*, which would have to occur, however, according to the nature of this concept.

That is, if a concept is *given* a priori as applicable in the world of sense (such as the concept of causality, for example), the very proof that it is given ensures its objective validity. But even if it is only *constructed* a priori, as, for example, the concept of a triangle, or even that of a Pegasus, its construction in space assures it immediately of this reality; and the judgment 'that is a triangle,' or 'that is a Pegasus,' means nothing more than 'that is the presentation of a concept that I have constructed for myself.' It is presupposed in such a judgment that nothing more belongs to the reality of the concept than the concept itself, and that it alone is to be viewed as a sufficient ground for that which corresponds to it. In the concept of revelation constructed a priori, however, there is in addition something quite different from our concept of it which certainly is presupposed for its reality: namely, a concept in God that is similar to our own. The categorical judgment, 'that is a revelation,' does not mean merely, 'this appearance in the world of sense is a presentation of one of *my* concepts,' but rather, 'it is the presentation of a *divine* concept in conformity with one of *my* concepts.' In order to justify such a categorical judgment, i.e., in order to assure the concept [143]

[43] *Gesamtausgabe*, pp. 99–112 (§12).

of revelation a reality external to us, it would have to be possible
to prove that a concept of the same was present in God, and that a
certain appearance is the intended presentation thereof.

On the one hand, such a proof could be conducted a priori,
namely, by demonstrating from the concept of God the necessity
that he not only have this concept but also that he have willed to
effect a presentation of it – perhaps in the same way that we must
necessarily infer, from the requirement of the moral law that God
give eternity to finite beings so that they can satisfy its eternally
valid commandment, that the concept of the infinite duration of
finite moral beings is not only in God as a concept but that he must
also realize it outside of himself. Such a proof, which, as is evident
without any reminder, would be admittedly only subjective, but
nevertheless universally valid, would prove a great deal, and even
more than we wished, since it would justify us quite independently
of all experience in the world of sense in assuming the absolute
existence of a revelation, whether or not an appearance is given in
the world of sense corresponding to its concept. But we have already
seen above that such a proof is impossible. That is, we have only a
moral concept of God, given by pure practical reason. If a datum
were found in this concept that justified us in ascribing to God the
concept of revelation, this datum would at the same time be the one
that would yield the concept of revelation itself, and would yield it,
in fact, a priori. We have already looked around in vain above,
however, for such a datum of pure reason and therefore admitted
that this concept is a merely constructed one.

On the other hand, this proof could be conducted a posteriori,
namely, by demonstrating from the determinations of the appearance
given in nature that it can be effected in no other way than directly
by divine causality, and by it, in turn, in no other way than according to the concept of revelation. It would not really need to [144]
be demonstrated that such a proof infinitely exceeds the powers of
the human spirit, since the requirements of such a proof need only
be named in order to deter one from undertaking it. However, this,
too, was done abundantly above.[44]

But one might still believe, after renouncing the hope for a strict

---

[44] A footnote at this point in the first edition, which was omitted in the
second, is translated in the Appendix, p. 178 below. I. H. Fichte retains it
in the *Sämmtliche Werke* with the indication that it was omitted in the
second edition.

proof, that the unprovable proposition could at least be rendered probable. Probability emerges, namely, whenever one comes upon the series of grounds that ought to lead us to the sufficient ground for a certain proposition, yet without being able to show this sufficient ground itself as given, or likewise to show the one that is its sufficient ground as given, etc.; and the closer one is to this sufficient ground, the higher is the degree of probability. Now one could choose to search for this sufficient ground either a priori (by descending from the causes to the effects) or a posteriori (by ascending from the effects to the causes). In the first case one would [145] have to show, say, an attribute in God (if an additional determining ground that could not be demonstrated came into play) which would have to move him to realize the concept of a revelation,[45] perhaps not *in general* – for of course we found such an attribute in God in §7 above in his determination by the moral law to extend morality outside himself by every possible means – but rather *under the empirically given determinations* of this particular revelation. In a similar way, for example, one can surmise from the wisdom of God, according to the analogy of its way of operating here below (thus by connecting this a priori concept with an experience), that finite beings will endure with bodies, but with bodies becoming more and more refined; but one cannot prove it (because there might be contrary grounds that we do not know). Apart from the fact that our spirit is so arranged that probable grounds are not able a priori to ground in it the slightest assent, one will also never discover such a determination in God. Or, in the second case, one would have to remove all the possibilities that a certain event could be effected by anything except divine causality, down to perhaps one, or two, etc. For we certainly do come upon this series of grounds for assuming a divine causality for certain appearances in the world of sense. For, regarded theoretically, it certainly is the first ground for assuming the origin of a certain event by God's immediate operation if *we* are unable to explain its genesis from natural causes. But this is only the first member of a series, whose extension we do not know at all, and which in itself is in all probability inconceivable for us, and it consequently disappears into nothing before the infinite number of other possibilities. Hence we cannot even adduce probable grounds to warrant a categorical judgment that something is a revelation.

[45] The remainder of this sentence was added in the second edition.

Perhaps someone may still believe for a moment that this probability would be grounded if an alleged revelation were found [146] to agree with the criteria of revelation. Therefore, to begin with: if an alleged revelation were at hand in which we had found all the criteria of truth – what judgment concerning it would this justify? All these criteria are the moral conditions under which alone such an appearance could be effected by God in conformity with the concept of a revelation, and without which it could not; but they are by no means, conversely, the conditions of an effect that could be caused only by God in conformity with this concept. If they were the latter, then by excluding the causality of all other beings they would justify the judgment, 'that *is* revelation.' But since they are not the latter but only the former, they justify merely the judgment, 'that *may* be revelation'; that is, if it is presupposed that in God the concept of a revelation was present and that he willed to present it, there is nothing in the given appearance that could contradict the possible assumption that it is a presentation of this kind. By such an examination according to the criteria, therefore, it becomes merely problematic that anything at all could be a revelation; but this problematic judgment is also completely certain.

In this problematic judgment, namely, there are really two things being expressed. First, it is possible in general that God had the concept of a revelation and that he willed to present it – and this is already clear immediately from the conformity to reason of the concept of revelation, in which this possibility is assumed. And second, it is possible that this specific alleged revelation is a presentation thereof. Now the latter judgment can be pronounced concerning every appearance proclaimed as revelation before any examination, and in conformity with fairness, it must be pronounced – specifically in this sense: 'it is possible that it may possess the criteria of a revelation.' Here, namely (before examination), the problematic judgment is composed of two problematic judgments. But when this examination is completed, and the proclaimed revelation is found trustworthy by it, the first judgment is no [147] longer problematic but completely certain: the appearance possesses all the criteria of a revelation. One can now judge with complete certainty, therefore, without waiting for any further datum or fearing an objection from anywhere, 'it *may* be one.' What does result from examination according to the criteria, therefore, is what can result from them, not merely as probable but as certain: namely,

whether it *may* be of divine origin. Whether it *actually is*, however
– concerning this question, nothing at all follows from the examination, because it was not even the question in this undertaking.

After completion of this examination the mind arrives at a complete balance between the pro and the con with regard to a categorical judgment – or it ought to, at least, from a rational point of
view – still inclined to neither side but ready at the first slight
impetus to incline towards the one or the other. No impetus for a
negative judgment is conceivable that does not contradict reason:
neither a strict proof, nor one sufficient for a probable conjecture,
for the negative proof is just as impossible as the affirmative and on
precisely the same grounds; nor a determination of the faculty of
desire by the practical law, because the acceptance of a revelation
possessing all the criteria of divinity in no way contradicts this law.
(Of course, a determination of the lower faculty of desire by the
inclination is certainly conceivable, which could prejudice us against
acknowledging a revelation, and one may indeed assume without
making oneself guilty of uncharitableness that *for many a man* such
a determination is the reason why he will accept no revelation; but
such an inclination plainly contradicts practical reason.) Therefore,
an impetus for the affirmative judgment must be discoverable, or we
will have to remain always in this indecision. Since this impetus,
too, can be neither a strict proof nor one sufficient for a probable
conjecture, it must be a determination of the faculty of desire.

We have already been in this situation before with the [148]
concept of God. Our reason, which for everything conditioned
seeks the totality of conditions, led us in ontology to the concept of
the most real being, in cosmology to a first cause, in teleology to an
intelligent being, from whose concepts we could derive the
purposive connection which is necessarily to be assumed everywhere
in the world for our reflection. No cause whatsoever was found to
show why something external to us should not correspond to this
concept, but our theoretical reason was nevertheless unable to assure
it this reality through any means. Through the law of practical
reason, however, a final purpose was established for us for the sake
of the form of our will, whose possibility was conceivable for us only
on the presupposition of the reality of that concept. And since we
will this final purpose absolutely, and hence had to assume its possibility theoretically as well, we had simultaneously to assume also
its conditions, the existence of God and the infinite duration of all

moral beings. Thus, a concept whose validity was previously utterly problematic was realized here not by theoretical arguments but in order to determine the faculty of desire.

As far as the problem is concerned, we are in a quite similar situation here. That is, a concept is present in our mind which is perfectly conceivable merely as such; and after an appearance is given in the world of sense which possesses all the criteria of a revelation, absolutely nothing further is possible that could contradict the acceptance of its validity; but neither can any theoretical argument be shown which could justify us in assuming this validity. The appearance is therefore fully problematic. It soon becomes evident, however, that the solution of this problem could not parallel the solution of the problem above at every step. The concept of God, namely, was given a priori by our reason and as such was absolutely necessary for us; and we were therefore unable to reject at will the responsibility of our reason to decide something about the validity of this concept outside ourselves. For the concept [149] of a revelation, however, we have no such a priori datum to adduce, and hence it would be quite possible either not to have this concept at all or to dismiss the question about its validity outside of ourselves as completely useless. From the very fact that it is not given a priori, it follows directly that it will likewise be impossible to show any a priori determination of the will which determines us to assume its reality, because then, of course, this determination of the will would be the missing a priori datum. This becomes fully clear when one remembers that nothing further is required in order to conceive as possible the final purpose established for us a priori than to assume the existence of God and the endurance of finite moral beings. Nothing in the concept of a revelation has anything at all to do with these propositions according to their matter; rather, it presupposes them as already accepted for the purpose of its own possibility. It is rather a matter of accepting a certain form of the confirmation of these propositions. Hence, no impetus for accepting the validity of the concept of revelation can be derived from the determination of the higher faculty of desire by the moral law. But perhaps from a determination of the lower faculty of desire by the higher in conformity with the moral law?

That is, the moral law commands absolutely, without regard to the possibility or impossibility, in general or in particular cases, of having a causality in the world of sense. And by means of the

determination of the higher faculty of desire to will the good absolutely, which occurs thereby, the lower faculty, which is determinable
also by natural laws, is determined to will *the means* for producing this
good, at least in itself (in its sensuous nature). The higher faculty of
desire wills the purpose absolutely; the lower faculty wills the means
for doing it. Now, in accordance with the development of the
formal function of revelation that occurred in §8, which is also the
only one essential to it, it is a means for sensuous human beings in
the struggle of inclination against duty to secure the predominance
of the latter over the former, if they are permitted to represent the
legislation of the Most Holy for themselves under sensuous [150]
conditions. The representation in this case is that of a revelation.
Hence, under the above conditions the lower faculty of desire must
necessarily will the reality of the concept of revelation; and, since no
rational ground at all is opposed to it, this faculty determines the
mind to accept it as actually realized, i.e., to accept as proved that a
certain appearance is actually the intentional presentation of this
concept effected by divine causality, and to make use of it according
to this assumption.

A determination by the lower faculty of desire to will the reality
of a representation whose object one cannot produce himself is a
wish, whatever it may be caused by.[46] Hence, the acceptance of a
certain appearance as divine revelation is based on nothing more
than a wish. Now since such a procedure of believing something
because one's heart wishes it is in considerable, and not undeserved,
ill repute, we must add a few more words, while not to deduce its
legitimacy, at least to reject all objections to this procedure in the
present case.

If a mere wish is to justify us in assuming the reality of its object,
it must be based on the determination of the higher faculty of desire
by the moral law, and must have arisen by means of this determination. Assuming the reality of its object must facilitate the
exercise of our duties – and not merely this or that duty, but dutiful
behavior in general – and it must be possible to show that assuming
the contrary would impede this dutiful behavior in the subjects
doing the wishing, because only with a wish of this kind are we able
to adduce a reason why we want to assume anything at all about

---

[46] In the first edition the foregoing sentence reads as follows: 'A deter-
    mination of the lower faculty of desire, whatever it may be caused by, is a
    wish.'

the reality of its object instead of dismissing the question about it completely. It has already been sufficiently demonstrated above that such is the case with the wish for a revelation.

This criterion of the possibility of assuming what is wished merely for the sake of the wish must also combine with the second criterion, namely, the complete certainty that in making [151] this assumption we can never be convicted of an error, in which case the matter would be completely true *for us*; it would be just as good for us as though it involved no possibility of error at all. Now this occurs in the strictest sense in the acceptance of a revelation possessing all the criteria of divinity, i.e., in the assumption that a certain appearance is effected by immediate divine causality in conformity with the concept of a revelation. The error of this assumption can never be evident to us from its grounds or be proved to us, even if we increase in insight through all eternity. For in that case, since this assumption by no means belongs before the judgment seat of theoretical reason, one would have to be able to show that it contradicted practical reason – that is, that it contradicted the concept of God given by practical reason. But this contradiction would already have to be evident now, since the moral law is the same for all rational beings at every stage of their existence. Nor can such an error be proved by a subsequent experience, as is so often the case with other human wishes, which are usually directed to the future. For how indeed is the experience to be constituted that could instruct us that an effect fully in conformity with a possible concept in God is *not* effected by the causality of this concept? This is an obvious impossibility – and so would be even the experience which we would have to have in the case that the effect was divinely caused, and from whose absence we could infer that it was not.

The investigation has been pushed to a point beyond which it cannot proceed for us: up to the insight into the full possibility of a revelation, in general as well as in particular, by means of a definitely given appearance. The investigation is completely closed *for us* (all finite beings). We see with complete certainty at the end point of this investigation that absolutely no proof concerning the actuality of a revelation, either for it or against it, takes place, or will ever take place; and that no being will ever know how the fact of the matter stands in itself, except God alone. [152]

Finally, if one still wished to assume, perhaps, as the only way we could be instructed concerning this matter, that God himself might communicate it to us, this would be a new revelation, concerning whose objective reality the previous ignorance would arise, and we would again be at the same point where we were before.

It is completely certain from everything that has been said that no conviction of error is possible concerning this point, i.e., that *for us* no error whatsoever is possible concerning it, but that a determination of the faculty of desire impels us to declare ourselves for the affirmative judgment. Therefore, we can submit to this determination with complete certainty.*

---

* Let us clarify what has been said here about the conditions of the permission to believe something because the heart wishes it, by means of an example of the contrary. One might wish to prove, namely, the revival of the association with former friends in the future life out of the desire for good men disposed to friendship after this revival. With such a proof, however, one would surely not succeed. For although one could say, for example, that the accomplishment of many a difficult duty would be made easier for one who knows a dear friend to be in eternity by the thought that in so doing he more and more insures the enjoyment of blessedness with his departed friend, nevertheless pure morality would not be furthered at all by this means but rather mere legality, and it would accordingly be a futile endeavor to want to derive this wish from the determination of the higher faculty of desire by the moral law – quite apart from the fact that one can easily point to countless motives of this kind to which one would still hesitate to grant objective reality on that account. Indeed, the only wishes that might rightfully claim such a noble descent in general are the wish to be allowed to assume traces of the divine moral governance in the whole of nature in general, and above all in our own life, and the wish to accept a revelation in particular. As far as the second condition is concerned, grounds can already be surmised sufficiently in this world by analogy which could make such a reunion in the future life inappropriate: for example, perhaps the goal of a versatile education could make the association with a former friend, whose purpose for our growth is achieved, useless to us, or even harmful; or this friend's presence might be more necessary in other connections and more useful for the whole; or our own presence might be more necessary in other connections; and so on. The assumed reality of this wish corresponds merely to the last condition; [153] for in a duration without end this reunion, if it is bound to no definite point in this duration, can always still be expected, and hence experience can never contradict its reality. For this reason, therefore, no proof of the satisfaction of this wish is possible. And if there is no other proof (but there is one, which suffices only for a probable supposition, however), the human mind would have to restrict itself to *hope* concerning such satisfaction, i.e., it would have to limit itself to an inclination of judgment, motivated by a determination of the faculty of desire, towards one alternative in a matter which is recognized, however, to be problematic.

The circumstances are the same, moreover, regarding the irrefutability of

This acceptance of a revelation, then, since it is legitimately [153] based on a determination of the faculty of desire, is a *faith*, which we will call *formal, empirically conditioned faith*, in order to distinguish it from *pure rational faith* in God and immortality, which refers to something *material*. The difference between the two, and everything we still have to say about the former, will follow from a comparison of the determination of the mind in the one case and the other according to the order of the category headings.[47]

According to *quality*, namely, faith, in the first as well [154] as the second case, is a free acceptance, not forced by any arguments, of the reality of a concept which cannot be assured of this reality by any arguments: in the first case a given concept, in the second a constructed one; in the first case for the sake of a negative determination of the lower faculty of desire (§2) by the higher, in the second for the sake of a positive determination of it by means of that negative one.[48] These are differences which have already been indicated and whose consequences have already been developed. But here a new one appears as well. In pure rational faith, namely, it is merely assumed that an object in general external to us corresponds to a concept, that of God (for faith in immortality can be regarded as merely derived from the existence of God, and thus we

---

the immediate postulates of practical reason, the existence of God and the eternal endurance of moral beings. Our endurance, of course, is an object of immediate experience, but faith in endurance can never be refuted by experience; for if we do not exist, we have no experience at all. Likewise, as long as we endure as *ourselves*, i.e., as moral beings, faith in God cannot be overturned, either by arguments – since it is not based on theoretical grounds, and the eternally valid law of practical reason supports it – or by experience – since the existence of God can never become an object of experience; and so likewise from the lack of such an experience his non-existence can never be inferred. On precisely the same grounds, however, these propositions also can never become objects of *knowledge* but must remain objects of *faith* for all eternity. For we shall never have any grounds other than moral ones for the existence of God, since no others are possible, and we will be certain of our own existence at each of its points immediately through self-consciousness but can expect it for the future on no other grounds than moral ones.

[47] Cf. Kant, *Critique of Pure Reason*, p. 113 (B 106).
[48] In the first edition the last part of the foregoing sentence (after the semicolon) reads as follows: '... in the first case for the sake of a determination of the higher faculty of desire, in the second for the sake of a determination of the lower, occasioned by this determination of the higher.'

do not have to give it any special consideration here). In revealed faith, however, not only is this assumed but also that a certain datum corresponds to this concept. Thus in the latter faith the mind appears to go a step further and to make a bolder presumption, which ought to have a greater justification to adduce for itself. But this is due to the nature of the two concepts, and the step is actually not bolder in the latter than in the former. Namely, the concept of God is already given as fully determined a priori, that is, as far as it can be determined by us, and cannot be further determined by any experience nor by inferences from the existence that has been assumed. A realization of it can therefore do nothing more at all than assume the existence of an object corresponding to it; it can add nothing further to it, because this object can be determined only in this one way given a priori. In the concept of revelation, however, an experience yet to be given is conceived, which as such, and insofar as it is to be given, can by no means be determined a priori but must rather be assumed as determinable a posteriori in manifold ways. To accept it as realized means nothing else, and can mean nothing else, than to think of it as given and completely determined. [155] This complete determination, however, must be given by experience. Consequently, no assumption whatsoever of the reality of this concept in general (*in abstracto*) takes place; rather, it can be realized only by application to a definite appearance (*in concreto*), and nothing happens through this application except what happens in pure rational faith: it is assumed that something external to a concept that is present a priori corresponds to it. If one speaks of the *quantity* of faith, only a *subjective* quantity can be meant, because no faith claims objective validity, in which case it would not be faith. Now in this regard pure rational faith is universally valid for all finite rational beings, because it is based on an a priori determination of the faculty of desire by the moral law to will something necessarily and concerns an a priori concept given by pure reason. It cannot be forced upon anyone, to be sure, because it is based on a determination of freedom, but it can be required and expected of everyone.

It is evident at once that empirically conditioned faith cannot claim this universal validity. For it concerns in part a concept that is not given but constructed and is therefore not necessary in the human mind. Now if someone did not come upon this concept in general, neither could he accept a presentation of it, and we would thus presuppose this assumption in him in vain, since we cannot even presuppose with certainty its concept in him. In part, however, the determination of the mind to accept a presentation of this concept is caused only by a wish, which is based on an empirical need. Now if someone does not feel this need *in himself*, even if he should know historically that it is present in others, the wish to be permitted to accept a revelation can never arise in him, hence also no faith in one.

Only a single case is conceivable in which at least a passing [156] faith is possible even without feeling this need in oneself: namely, when someone not in need of a revelation himself is compelled to have an effect on the hearts of others who do need it through the representation of a revelation. The active wish in conformity with his duty to extend morality also outside himself according to his powers, combined with the conviction that this is possible for the given subjects only by means of this representation, will drive him to make use of it. He cannot use it with real energy without speaking as one who is himself convinced and who believes. To feign this faith would go against the truth and sincerity of the mind and thus would be morally impossible. The urgent feeling of a need for revealed faith which thereby arises in this situation will produce the faith itself in him, at least for as long as this feeling lasts, even if he should perhaps put this representation gradually aside again after he has cooled down.*

It follows from what has been said, therefore, that faith in revelation not only cannot be forced but also cannot even be required or expected of everyone.

Just as faith in revelation is possible only on two conditions, namely, that one partly wants to be good and partly needs the representation of a revelation having occurred as a means for producing the good in himself,** so likewise unbelief in regard [157]

---

* Every teacher of religion, who does not perhaps personally make use of representations taken from revelation but who does combine active feeling for his vocation with honesty (which is saying not a little), will perhaps concede to us, even if not publicly yet at least in his heart, that this is not an empty sophistry but is also confirmed by experience, especially when giving public speeches to the people.

It occurs by means of inspiration by the imagination; and this circumstance must not make anyone suspicious of the matter, since revelation in general, of course, can and should operate only by means of this vehicle. [The final sentence of this footnote was added in the second edition.]

** Such were also the maxims of Jesus. As far as the former is concerned:

to it can have two causes: either, namely, that one has no good will
at all and thus hates and rejects everything that prompts us to good
and has the appearance of wanting to limit our inclinations; or,
that one with the best of wills just does not need the support of a
revelation in order to set him going. The former condition of the
soul is profound moral corruption; the latter is real strength, if only
it is based not on the natural weakness of our inclinations, or on a
kind of life that destroys them, but rather on effective respect of the
good for its own sake. And one may say this without fear of thereby
taking anything away from the dignity of revelation, because in
really dominant love of the good, without which no faith at all is
possible, it is not to be feared that someone will reject it as long as
he is still aware of some good effect that it has in itself. Only the
fruits are able to show from which of the two causes the unbelief
arises in a particular subject.

In order to reject an over-hasty conclusion, however, we note here
that although faith in revelation makes no claim to universal
validity, the critique of its concept nevertheless does. For the latter
has to ground nothing but the absolute possibility of a revelation in
its concept, as well as that something corresponding to it may be
assumed. And it does so from principles that are a priori, hence
universally valid. Everyone is therefore required by this critique to
grant not only that a revelation is possible in general but also that
an appearance actually given in the world of sense which possesses
all the criteria of a revelation *may* be one. With this, however, [158]
it must rest satisfied, and with this everyone can and must from a
rational point of view rest satisfied who feels no need to make use of
it either in himself or in others. It is necessitated by this critique,
however, to grant to those who believe in revelation the conformity
of their faith to reason and to leave them in utterly serene and
undisturbed possession and practice thereof.

As far as *relation* is concerned, pure rational religion refers to
something material; revealed faith, however, refers merely to a

if any man *wills* to do the will of him who sent me, he shall know [157]
whether the doctrine is from God [John 7.17]; and on the contrary, Every
one who does evil hates the light, and does not come to the light [John
3.20]. As far as the latter is concerned: those who are strong have no
need of a physician, but those who are sick; I have not come to call the
righteous, but sinners to repentance [cf. Luke 5.31–2] – which sayings I
do not take as irony.

definite form of this material, which is given a priori and is already presupposed as assumed. This difference, which is sufficiently clear from everything said up to here, induces us merely to make the remark here that one who does not accept this definite form of a revelation not only does not necessarily deny the material, God and immortality, but does not even prejudice the belief in them in himself, if he is able to conceive of them just as well outside of this form and to use them to determine his will.

As far as *modality* is concerned, finally, pure rational religion expresses itself apodictically according to the presupposition of the possibility of the final purpose of the moral law. That is, once it is assumed that absolute right is possible, it is utterly necessary for us to think that there is a God and that moral beings endure eternally. Faith in revelation, however, can only express itself categorically: 'a certain appearance *is* revelation'; not 'it must necessarily be revelation' – because however certain it is that no error in this judgment can be demonstrated to us, yet the contrary always remains possible in itself.

§15

General Overview of This Critique[49]

Before any investigation of the concept of revelation was possible, this concept had to be defined, at least provisionally. And we did not fare as well here as in the case of given concepts in pure [159] philosophy, which we trace back to their origin and, as it were, see them arise; on the contrary, this concept proclaims itself merely as empirical and, even though its possibility a priori follows from closer investigation, it does not at least appear to be able to adduce for itself a datum a priori. For this reason, we needed *at first* only to listen to the linguistic usage. This took place in §5. But since this concept is rational only in relation to religion, as could already be surmised provisionally but was completely provable in §5, a deduction of religion in general had to be premised for the purpose of deriving the concept to be investigated from its higher concept (§§2, 3, 4).[50]

After this provisional definition of the concept, the questions to be investigated were whether it is to be subjected to a philosophical critique at all, and before what tribunal its subject matter is to be brought. The first depended on whether the concept is possible a priori, and the second had to follow from an actual deduction a priori from those principles from which it could be derived, since every concept obviously belongs under the field of that principle from which it is derived. This deduction was actually given in [160] §§5, 6, and 7; and from this it became clear that this concept belongs before the tribunal of practical reason. The second topic, which must be subjected to a strict examination, is therefore this deduction a priori, because with its possibility the possibility of any critique of this concept in general and the correctness of the one given, along

---

[49] In the first edition this title reads, 'Concept of This Critique in General.' *Gesamtausgabe*, pp. 113–16 (§13).

[50] A continuation of this paragraph in the first edition, omitted in the second, is translated in the Appendix, p. 178 below. I. H. Fichte retains it in the *Sämmtliche Werke* as a 'supplement from the first edition.'

with the conformity to reason of the criticized concept itself, stands or falls.

Since it was found in this deduction that the concept under investigation has no datum a priori to show but rather anticipates one a posteriori, the possibility of this required datum had to be shown in experience – but only its possibility. This took place in §8. In the examination in this chapter the question is merely whether an empirical need for a revelation, which is the required datum, has, perhaps, not actually been exhibited but simply correctly indicated, and whether from the empirical determinations of mankind the possibility has been derived that such a need might arise.

In addition, in §9 the physical possibility of a revelation was shown, about which as such no question could arise at all, not so much for the sake of a systematic necessity but more for the purpose of making still more plausible the proposition that the investigation of the possibility of a revelation by no means belongs before the forum of theoretical reason, a proposition that the deduction of its concept already makes clear.

After completion of this investigation it must be completely clear that the concept of revelation in general is not only conceivable in itself but also is able, in the event that an empirical need should arise, to anticipate something outside itself that corresponds to itself. But since this correspondent is to be an appearance in the world of sense and must be *given* (cannot be *constructed*), the human spirit can then do nothing more than apply this concept to such an appearance; and the critique can do nothing more than guide it in so doing, i.e., set the conditions under which such an application is possible. These conditions were developed in §§10, 11, and 12. Since [161] they are nothing more than the determinations of the concept of revelation itself, resulting from an analysis, the only questions in their examination are whether they actually proceed from this concept and whether they are all specified. Chapter 13 seeks to facilitate the examination of the last point.

Since, however, it obviously follows from the nature of this concept that its actual application to a given experience is always merely arbitrary and not based on any necessity of reason, it had still to be shown in §14 what this application in general is based on and to what extent it conforms to reason. This deduction of the conformity to reason of this procedure for dealing with the concept of revelation is also in need of a special examination.

From this brief overview it becomes clear that the critique of revelation should be carried out from principles a priori; for in the investigation of the empirical datum for the concept of revelation, it is obliged merely to show its possibility. Hence it becomes clear that the critique makes legitimate claim to universal validity, unless an error can be demonstrated in it at any of the points indicated. But should such an error have been made in the present treatment of this critique, as is surely to be expected, it should be easy to correct it and to establish a universally valid critique of all revelation – provided only that the course of a possible critique has been correctly indicated, which must soon become apparent, especially through mutual efforts.

Through this critique the possibility of a revelation as such, and in particular the possibility of believing in a definite, given one, is now fully secured, provided it has been confirmed in advance before the tribunal of its particular critique. Through this critique all objections against it are laid to rest forever, and all conflict about it is settled for all time.* Through it, all criticism of every particular given revelation is founded, because it establishes the [162] general principles of every such critique on the basis of the criteria of all revelation. After first settling the historical question of *what* a given revelation really teaches – which in particular cases might easily be the hardest question – it becomes possible to decide with complete certainty whether a revelation could be of divine origin or not, and, in the first case, to believe in it without any fear of an interference of any kind.

---

* This conflict is based on an antinomy of the concept of revelation and is fully dialectical. Acknowledgment of a revelation is not possible, says the one part; acknowledgment of a revelation is possible, says the second. [162] And thus expressed, the two propositions contradict each other directly. But if the first is thus defined: acknowledgment of a revelation on theoretical grounds is impossible; and the second: acknowledgment of a revelation for the sake of determining the faculty of desire, i.e., a faith in revelation, is possible; then they do not contradict each other but can both be true, as indeed they are according to our critique.

Concluding Remark[51]

It is a very common observation that everything that is speculation, or looks like it, has very little impact on the human mind. One is, at most, pleasantly occupied thereby; one puts up with the result because one can find no objection to it but would likewise find no harm in it if it turned out differently. Moreover, one thinks and acts with regard to practical matters as before, so that the proposition founded on speculation seems to lie in the soul like unemployed capital without earning any interest and one is in no way aware of its presence. So it has been from time immemorial with the speculations of idealists and skeptics. They have thought like no one else and acted like everyone else.

Even if the present speculation does not necessarily have any practical consequences for life (as it would like to have, however, if it asserted itself), the subject with which it deals no doubt guarantees that it will nevertheless not be received so coldly and indifferently in view of its interest. There is, namely, in the human soul a necessary interest in everything having to do with religion; and this can be explained quite naturally from the fact that religion became possible only through determination of the faculty of desire. This theory is therefore confirmed by universal experience, and a person might almost wonder why from this experience he had not arrived at it long ago by himself. If someone were to deny another immediately [164] certain proposition, e.g., that only one straight line is possible between two points, we would sooner laugh at him and feel sorry for him than get angry at him. And if the mathematician should happen to get excited about it, this could only arise either from displeasure with himself because he cannot immediately convince the other of his error or from the suspicion that this obstinate denial is based on the ill will of wanting to irritate him (hence on something immoral as well). But this resentment would nevertheless be of a quite different kind from the one that seizes everyone – and most of all the least educated person – whenever anyone denies the

51 *Gesamtausgabe*, pp. 116–23.

existence of God or the immortality of the soul. This resentment is
mixed with fear and loathing, clearly signifying that we view this
faith as a cherished possession and the one who threatens to disturb
us in this possession as our personal enemy. For this interest extends
itself proportionately farther the more ideas we are able to relate to
religion and to bring into connection with it; and we would therefore consider carefully in deciding whether predominant tolerance
is a very estimable trait in a soul in which it cannot be based on long
and persistent reflection. On the other hand, the severe antipathy
that prejudices us against representations which we perhaps once
took to be holy, but concerning which we have become convinced
or persuaded with increasing maturity that they are not, can likewise
be explained from this same interest. Indeed, we recall other dreams
of our earlier years – as, for example, that of a disinterested willing-
ness of human beings to help, of an Arcadian pastoral innocence,
etc. – with a glad, but melancholy, remembrance of the years when
we were still able to dream so pleasantly, although the contrary, and
the experiences by which we may have been warned about it, cannot
possibly be pleasant in themselves. For a long time, however, we
recall with chagrin the delusions of the kind indicated above, [165]
and it requires much time and reflection to become indifferent
about them as well. This phenomenon is by no means to be explained
by the obscure representation of the harm resulting from such ideas
(since we view even the obvious harm itself with more equanimity),
but rather merely from the fact that the holy is cherished by us and
we view every admixture of an extraneous ingredient as a desecra-
tion of it.[52] This interest, finally, becomes evident even in the fact
that we do not boast so much about any other kind of knowledge as
about presumed better insights into religion, as though this were the
greatest honor, and in the fact that we so much enjoy communi-
cating these insights to others on the sure supposition that this subject is universally interesting (unless, perhaps, good etiquette has
banned such conversations; even though the fact that they had to be
banned seems to indicate a universal inclination towards them).

[52] The first edition contains a longer version of the foregoing sentence, as
follows: 'This phenomenon is to be explained neither by the obscure
representation ... nor by the influence of evil beings outside us, as does,
for instance, a certain author – who, however, seems since to have changed
his opinion – but rather ...' The 'certain author,' to whom reference was
dropped in the second edition, is not identified.

As certain as we may be from this side, therefore, that the present investigation will be received not wholly without interest, we have to fear that this very same interest may turn against us and disturb the reader in the calm consideration and weighing of the arguments if he should happen to anticipate, or should actually find, that the result turns out to be not wholly in accordance with his preconceived opinion. Thus it seems to be a not wholly futile task even at this point to investigate – wholly without regard for substantiating the result, and just as though we had not followed a path prescribed a priori which would necessarily have to have led us to it, but rather as though it had depended entirely on us how it would turn out – to investigate whether we might have had cause to wish for a more favorable result, or whether the present one is in general the most advantageous that we could have promised ourselves – in short, to investigate the same thing wholly without regard for its truth but merely from the aspect of its utility.

Here, however, we encounter at the very beginning those who will say, in the best opinion of the world, that nothing at all [166] intelligent can come out of an investigation of this kind, and that it would have been better to abstain completely from the present investigation. These people absolutely do not want to see anything connected with revelation reduced to principles; every examination of it they shun, fear, and reject. Yet if they want to be candid, they will admit that they themselves have a poor opinion of their faith, and they may decide for themselves whether they prefer the respect and indulgence of those who view the case for revelation as having already been fully and finally tried and lost on every appeal and who think that a man who would act honorably should no longer concern himself with it, who even think it a poor feat of heroism to destroy it completely, and that one may surely grant this basically innocent plaything – presumably out of charitable indulgence – to those who have simply set their hearts on it. Nevertheless, we are not really concerned with these people here, since probably not one of them will read this work, but only with those who permit an examination of revelation.

According to our intention the present examination should be the strictest possible. So what have we lost by it? What have we gained? Which of these has predominance?

We have lost all our prospects for conquests, objective as well as subjective. We can no longer hope through help of a revelation to penetrate into the realm of the supersensuous and to bring back who-knows-what kind of spoils from there. We must rather resign ourselves to be satisfied with what was given to us once and for all as our complete equipment. Neither may we hope any longer to subjugate others and to force them to take in fee from us their share in the common inheritance or in this supposed new acquisition. We must rather restrict ourselves to our own business, each one for himself.

We have gained complete peace and security in our [167] possession: security from those importunate benefactors who force their gifts upon us without our knowing what to do with them; security from those other disturbers of the peace who would like to spoil for us what they do not know how to use themselves. We have only to remind both of their poverty, which they have in common with us, and in view of which we differ only in that we know it and adapt our consumption accordingly.

Then have we lost more or gained more? Certainly the loss of the insights into the supersensuous for which we had hoped seems to be a substantial loss, which cannot be replaced and which we can ill afford. It would be easier to console ourselves about it, however, if closer investigation should yield that we do not need such insights for anything at all, and indeed, that we cannot even be sure whether we really possess them or whether we are in fact deceiving ourselves about them.

It has now been proved sufficiently that there is no objective certainty about the reality of any ideas of the supersensuous but only a faith in them. All faith developed so far is based on a determination of the faculty of desire (on a determination of the higher faculty in the case of the existence of God and the soul's immortality; on a determination of the lower by the higher in the case of the concept of providence and revelation) and in turn facilitates this determination reciprocally. It has clearly been shown that no further ideas are possible in whose reality a direct or indirect determination by the practical law would move us to believe. So the only question remaining here is whether a faith is not possible which does *not* arise through such a determination and does *not* facilitate it in turn. In the first case, it must be easy to decide whether the faith actually exists *in concreto*; namely, it must follow from the practical consequences that this faith must necessarily produce as a way of facilitating the determination of the will. In the latter case, however, where no such practical consequences are possible, it appears difficult to determine anything solid about it, since the faith is [168] something merely subjective, and it fully appears that nothing is left for us to do but to believe every honest man at his word when he says to us, I believe this, or I believe that. Nevertheless, it is perhaps possible to ascertain something even about this case. For it is surely not to be denied that a person often persuades others, and just as often himself, that he believes something when he simply has nothing against it and leaves it quietly in its place. Nearly all historical faith is of this kind, unless it happens to be based on a determination of the faculty of desire, such as the faith in the historical element in a revelation, or the faith of a professional historian, which is inseparable from respect for his occupation and from the importance that he is bound to place on his painstaking investigations, or the faith of a nation in an event that supports its national pride. Reading about the events and activities of beings who have the same concepts and the same passions that we have is a pleasant way of occupying ourselves; and it contributes something to the increasing of our enjoyment if we may assume that people of this kind actually lived, and we assume it all the more firmly the more the story interests us, the more similarity it has to our events or our way of thinking. But we would also have little objection, especially in some cases, if everything were mere fiction. Even if it is not true, it is well concocted, we would think. How, then, is one to come to some certainty about oneself in this matter?

The only true test of whether one really accepts something is whether he acts accordingly, or would act accordingly should the case for applying it arise. Concerning opinions which have in themselves no practical application, nor could have, an experiment nevertheless takes place every time a person asks himself conscientiously whether he would be willing to stake a portion of his wealth, or all of it, or his life, or his freedom on the correctness of a certain [169] opinion if it should be possible to decide something certain about it. Thereupon he gives artificially a practical application to an opinion which has in itself no practical consequences. If in this manner it should be proposed to someone that he bet his entire wealth that Alexander the Great did not live, he could perhaps accept this bet unhesitatingly, because with utter sincerity he might still dimly think that those experiences which could decide this issue are simply no longer possible. But if a similar bet should perhaps be proposed to the same person that no Dalai Lama exists, with the offer to verify the matter on the spot by direct experience, he may perhaps want to be more reflective about it and thereby betray that he is not utterly settled in his faith on this point. Now if a person should propose to himself just as substantial a bet about faith in supersensuous things whose concept is not given a priori by pure practical reason and which can thus have in themselves no practical consequences at all, it would very easily be possible for him to discover from the fact that he would refuse it that he hitherto had not had faith in them but had only persuaded himself that he had it. Even if a person should actually accept this bet, however, he could still not be sure whether his mind had not quite dimly recollected that it still was by no means necessary to let itself be caught at its guile, since nothing at all is hazarded in such a bet because the fact (in ideas of this kind) cannot be decided in eternity either by arguments or by experiences. Therefore, even if it could not be proved that no faith at all is possible in the reality of such ideas, nevertheless one thing follows easily from this: It is never possible even to make up one's own mind whether one has this faith in general, which is precisely the same as if it were not possible in general and in itself. From this situation we have to judge whether we have cause to be very embarrassed about the loss of our hope of gaining expanded [170] insights into the supersensuous world by means of a revelation.

As far as the second loss is concerned, we ask everyone to answer before his conscience the question, for what purpose he really wants to have a religion: whether for the purpose of exalting himself over others and boasting before them in order to satisfy his pride, his lust for power over consciences, which is much worse than the lust for power over bodies; or for the purpose of forming himself into a better human being.

In the meantime, we need a religion for others as well, partly to disseminate pure morality among them; but in this case it may only be proved that this could occur in no other way than the one indicated, so we will of course gladly avoid every other way if we are serious about it. And we need a religion partly, if we should be unable to do this, in order to make sure at least of their legality – a wish which in itself is quite legitimate. And as far as the possibility of thereby achieving it is concerned, there is surely nothing easier than frightening the person who is afraid of the dark anyway, in order by this means to lead him wherever one wants and to induce him as much as one wants to let his mortal body burn in hope of paradise. But if it is shown that morality would necessarily be destroyed completely by such a manipulation of religion, a person will of course quite gladly give up a power to which he has no right, especially since this legality is achieved far more surely and at least without harmful consequences for morality by other means.[53]

This, then, would be the account of our loss. Now let us contrast the gain.

We gain complete security in our possession. We may use our faith for our improvement without fear that it will be stolen from us by any kind of sophistry, without anxiety that someone may ridicule it, without timidity before the chastisement of idiocy and imbecility. Every refutation must be false; we can know that [171] a priori. Every derision must redound upon its author.

We gain complete freedom of conscience, not from coercion of conscience by physical means, which never really happens – since external coercion can force us to confess what it will with our lips but never to think something corresponding to it in our hearts – but rather from the infinitely harder coercion of conscience by moral oppressions and vexations, by exhortations, entreaties, threats, and who-knows-what kind of nasty evils that people force on our minds. By this means the soul is brought to an anxious fear and torments itself until it finally brings itself to lie to itself and to feign faith within itself – an hypocrisy that is far more terrible than utter un-belief, because the latter corrupts the character only as long as it lasts but the former destroys it without hope of ever improving, so that such a person can never again form the slightest respect or trust in himself. This is bound to be the consequence of the method which wants to base faith on fear and terror, and only on this extorted faith to base morality (a secondary matter, which may do well enough if it is to be had, but failing which, faith alone is surely able to see us through). And this would indeed have always been the consequence if people had set about it consistently and human nature were not too well arranged by its creator to let itself be so perverted.

[53] In the first edition the last part of this sentence reads as follows: '... especially since this legality, and everything that is counted as part of it in some states, is achieved far more surely and at least without harmful consequences for morality by other means than large standing armies, military and penal execution, and the like.'

According to the standard of these principles, the only way – a way that Christianity plainly prescribes as well – to produce faith in the hearts of men would be this one: first to make the good really esteemed and valued by them by developing the moral feeling, and thereby to arouse in them the resolve to become good men; then to let them feel their weakness everywhere, and only then to [172] offer them the prospect of the support of a revelation, and they would believe before one had called to them, Believe!

And now the decision about where the predominance lies, whether on the side of the gain or that of the loss, may be left to the heart of each reader, with the assurance of the incidental advantage that each person will come to know his own heart better from the judgment that he passes on this matter.

APPENDIX

Passages omitted in the Second Edition

ORIGINAL BEGINNING OF § 3
(= §2 in the First Edition)
[See p. 60 above, notes 14 and 15.]

Through the legislation of reason, simply a priori and without relation to any purpose, a final purpose is proposed: namely, *the highest good*, i.e., the highest moral perfection united with the highest Happiness. We are determined necessarily by the commandment to *will* this final purpose; but according to theoretical laws, under which all of our knowledge stands, we can know neither its possibility nor its impossibility. If we therefore wanted to hold it to be impossible, we would partly, even with regard to theoretical laws, be assuming something without basis, and partly we would be placing ourselves in the self-contradiction of *willing something impossible*. Or if we wanted just to leave its possibility or impossibility in its place, assuming neither the one nor the other, this would be a complete indifference that cannot coexist with our serious willing of this final purpose. So nothing is left for us but *to believe* in its possibility – i.e., to assume it not because we are forced by objective reasons but rather because we are moved by the necessary determination of our faculty of desire to will its actuality. If we assume the possibility of this final purpose, we cannot without the greatest inconsistency avoid also assuming all the conditions which alone make it conceivable for us. The highest morality united with the highest Happiness is supposed to be possible. But the highest morality is* possible only in a being whose practical faculty is actually determined (not just *supposed* to be determined) wholly and solely by the moral law; such a being must also simultaneously possess the highest Happiness if the final purpose of the

---

* If we express ourselves here categorically and in what follows in terms of necessity, we do not by any means want thereby to give our propositions out to be objectively valid and necessary in themselves. Rather, we are saying only that *we, assuming the possibility of the highest good according to our subjective constitution*, must also conceive this possibility as necessarily true. We are thus speaking only of a *hypothetical, subjective* necessity, to which we want herewith to call attention once and for all and as valid for this entire treatise.

moral law is conceived as having been achieved in him. So the proposition, 'there exists a being in whom the highest moral perfection is united with the highest blessedness,' is fully identical with the proposition, 'the final purpose of the moral law is possible.' But since we cannot at all conceive what the highest blessedness of such a being might consist of and how it might become possible, its concept is still not thereby extended in the least. In order to be able to extend it, we must consider other moral beings whom we know – namely, ourselves. That is, we ourselves, finite rational beings, are also supposed to be determined solely by the moral law in respect to our rational nature; our sensuous nature, however, which has a great influence on our Happiness, is determined not by this law but by wholly other laws. To be sure, our reason is supposed to produce in us the first part of the highest good; it is unable to realize the second, however, because that on which it depends does not come under its legislation. Now unless this second part, and thus the entire highest good with regard to finite rational beings, is to be wholly given up as impossible – which, however, would contradict the determination of our will – we must, just as surely as we must assume that the furthering of the final purpose of the moral law in us is possible, also assume that the sensuous nature is under the jurisdiction of some rational nature, though not our own, and that there is a being who is not simply himself independent of the sensuous nature but rather on whom it depends. And since this is to be dependence on the moral law, this being must be determined wholly by the moral law. But such a being is the God whom one assumes immediately when one assumes the possibility of the final purpose of the moral law. There must be a *completely holy, completely blessed, omnipotent being*. This being must, . . .

ORIGINAL BEGINNING OF §6
(= §4 in the First Edition)

[See p. 91 above, notes 21 and 22.]

The concept of revelation is, therefore, a concept of an effect produced by God in the sensuous world by means of supernatural causality, by which he proclaims himself as moral lawgiver. The question arises: is this concept possible a priori, or is it of merely empirical origin? If it is the latter, it is useless to *philosophize* about it – i.e., to want to decide something a priori about its possibility, reality, presumptions, and warrants. In that case we must calmly wait for experience and expect all instruction about the concept only from it. But even in the first fleeting glance at this concept we see so much in it that appears to indicate to us its a priori origin: the concept of God, that of a supernatural, that of a moral legislation – all concepts that are only possible a priori through the practical reason. Its a priori origin is surely not thereby proved, but it does hold out some hope to us that we might well find it by searching for it in this sphere – especially since it is immediately clear from the analysis of it that if it relies on nothing more than experience it is certainly false and surreptitiously obtained, since it promises us a view into the sphere of the supernatural, which is not possible by means of any experience or on the basis of any experience. Now if it is to be a priori, it must be capable of deduction a priori from concepts – and specifically, since it is plainly not a natural concept, from ideas of pure reason, . . .

ORIGINAL BEGINNING OF §7
(= §5 in the First Edition)

[See p. 95 above, note 23.]

According to the concept of revelation, God should proclaim himself to us as moral lawgiver by means of a supernatural effect in the sensuous world. Thus we are to be first instructed by this effect that God is moral lawgiver. Only from this appearance given in experience are we able to abstract the concept of it, of its supernatural cause, and of its intent – i.e., the concept of a revelation. At first glance this is what one thinks he can infer; but we now have to test the correctness of this inference.

Before proceeding, we need once more to recall that the question here is by no means whether incidental causes can be given a posteriori, and whether the required supernatural effect in the sensuous world and everything connected with it might be one such cause for developing that which was already in our reason a priori and raising us to clear consciousness of it. In this case we learn nothing from experience but are only led by it to recall what we know. And neither is the question whether we can proceed from experience by false pretenses, by not noticing that we are supplementing what we experience with what was already given to us a priori, to the concept of a revelation and think that a certain event is one. Rather, the question is whether this concept, and a rational assumption that a given appearance corresponds to it, is possible by means of experience and on the basis of it, in a rational manner and in accordance with the laws of thought.

We want to assume the case in which it might be said to some person in an appearance, in a dream, or the like: 'there is a God, and he is moral lawgiver.' Now on the one hand, this person may simply not yet have any concept of God and of duty, i.e., he may have no practical reason – and if we want him to *learn* those truths only through this proclamation, we must make this assumption; for if we grant him the legislation of practical reason, he already has those concepts a priori and necessarily, obscure and undeveloped though they may be. But then he could also not get them through this proclamation, for they are concepts that are not contained in any natural philosophy. He would simply understand nothing of what he heard; for him they would be concepts from another world, as indeed they are. On the other hand, assuming that this person had practical capability a priori, he would accordingly have the idea of duty and of God and would merely be assured by this appearance that God really is his moral lawgiver, just as he had already supposed and wished a priori. Then from the given experience he would have to be able to infer with certainty its supernatural origin – in fact, its origin from God. In other words, all experience is to be judged according to natural laws, and in the case at hand the problem is to find its cause from the constitution of its effect. Since the effect would be given in the sensuous world, he would be obliged by the laws of thought to seek the cause in the very same world. Now supposing that he were not to find it here, that he were to find no law of nature by which the causality in this case could have been determined, he could infer nothing more from this than that this law lay too deep for *him* to investigate. But should he want to infer as follows: 'because *I* do not find the cause of this appearance in the sensuous world, it is not there at all but in the supernatural world' – he would thereby make the first mistake, by ascribing to himself a complete knowledge of natural laws, which, even supposing that he had it, he could still never prove either to others or to himself, as would, however, be required for rational conviction. Should he want further to infer: 'now since the cause of this appearance is to be posited in a being of the supernatural world, it is to be posited in God' – he would make the second mistake, by overlooking without any proof the causality of all conceivable beings in the supernatural world, i.e., all beings who through freedom can become a cause in the sensuous world, and by quite arbitrarily assuming God to be the cause of this appearance. Such an inference contradicts the laws of thought; but the possibility that the concept of revelation could arise a posteriori would presuppose such an inference; consequently, this concept is not possible a posteriori from a rational point of view.

It may well be that the above inference has been made more than once, that it is even in fact the basis of alleged divine revelations, indeed, that by means of it the idea of revelation in general first became known among men. All those, however, who made the inference assumed something without proof; and if we are able to discover no other origin for this concept, we must give it up as impossible and wholly contradictory to the laws of thought.

Since it is not possible a posteriori, it must be so a priori if it is to be so at all – and specifically, since a practical intention was predicated in it, from principles of pure reason – and this must be shown by a deduction of these principles.

That is, if finite moral beings, . . .

[See p. 144 above, note 40.]

It cannot be demonstrated, of course, that even if one accepted these sensuous presentations as objectively valid this would result directly in contradictions with morality, as would result from an objective anthropomorphizing of God. The cause thereof is the following: God is totally supersensuous; the concept of him arises purely and only out of pure reason a priori; it cannot be adulterated without simultaneously adulterating the principles of the latter.

The concept of immortality, however, is not derived purely from reason but rather presupposes a possible experience, namely, that there are finite rational beings whose actuality is not given immediately by pure reason. A sensuous representation of immortality could therefore claim to derive its objective validity either from the *finitude* of moral beings or from their *moral nature*. If the former should occur, it would not contradict the principles of all morality, because such a proof would have to be conducted from theoretical principles, which do not encounter moral principles.

If the latter should occur, the proof would have to be conducted from attributes that were common to all moral natures, hence also God. Therefore, God himself would thereby be bound to the laws of sensibility, from which all kinds of contradictions with morality would result. Of course, it does not contradict morality that *I*, man with an earthly body, could not endure at all except with such a body, [138] and in fact with precisely the body that I have here; that this body, perhaps for the sake of a cause lying in its nature, would first have to decay for a time and then be able once again to be united with my soul; and so on. But it would contradict morality to say that God is bound to this condition, because his nature would then be determined by something other than the moral law. Since this point can easily be left undecided in asserting an objective validity of the concept of resurrection, neither does anything contrary to morality follow from this assertion in itself.

But such an objective assertion cannot be justified and proved by anything. Not by divine authority, for a revelation is based only on the authority of God as the Holy One; but such a condition of our immortality cannot be derived from his moral nature, because otherwise it would also have to be directly derivable from pure reason a priori. A revelation has nothing at all to do with theoretical proofs, and as soon as it engages in them it is no longer religion but physics – and may no longer demand faith but must force conviction, and this conviction is then valid no further than the proofs go. For resurrection, however, no theoretical proof is possible, because in this concept something supra-mundane is supposed to be inferred from something sensuous.

[See p. 149 above, note 44.]

* Meanwhile it cannot be denied that there is in human nature a universal, irresistible propensity to infer from the incomprehensibility of an event according to natural laws its existence through direct divine causality. This propensity arises from the responsibility of our reason to search for the totality of conditions for everything conditioned. And this totality is present at once, and we have no further trouble in searching for these conditions, if, as soon as we can no longer get on easily with the search for them, we are permitted to turn at once to the uncon-ditioned (or the first condition of everything conditioned). Since this overhaste to close the unbounded series of conditions, however, always leaves the door wide open to every fanaticism and nonsense, one has to proceed without leniency against it at every opportunity. But if it is already decided tentatively that the explanation of a certain event from divine causality will have no detrimental, but even favorable, conse-quences for morality – might one not be permitted in this single case to relent somewhat from the strictness, so necessary otherwise, against our presumptuous reason and to leave to a beneficent faith this one addi-tional point of contact in the human spirit, even though it is demon-strably obtained on false pretenses?

[See p. 162 above, note 50.]

The first object in the investigation of this critique is therefore whether the concept of revelation is defined according to the linguistic usage of all times and all peoples that boasted or boast of a revelation; and this is necessary because it is not a given but a constructed concept. For if the opposite should be the result, then – however correctly and thoroughly the concept established and invented by us contrary to linguistic usage might be investigated – this entire work would be only a game, a sophistical exercise, but of no essential use. But linguistic usage is not to be heard beyond the provisional definition of the concept, i.e., beyond the specification of its genus and its specific difference; for otherwise the possibility of any critique would be abolished and error would be sanctioned and perpetuated.

Glossary

The spelling of German words has been modernized.

ableiten: to derive
Achtung: respect
anerkennen: to acknowledge
angenehm: pleasant
ankündigen: to proclaim
Anmassung: presumption
annehmen: to assume *or* accept
Anschauung: intuition
Antrieb: stimulus
Befehl: command
Befugnis: warrant
Begehr: desire
Begehrungsvermögen: faculty of desire
Begierde: desire
Begriff: concept
bestimmen: to determine *or* define
darstellen: to present
Dasein: existence
dauern: to endure
Einbildungskraft: imagination
Empfindung: sensation
Endursache: final cause
Endzweck: final purpose
Entäusserung: alienation
Erkenntnis: knowledge *or* cognition
Erkenntnisvermögen: faculty of cognition
Erscheinung: appearance
Existenz: existence
Fürwahrhalten: assent
Gebot: commandment
Gegenstand: object

gelten: to be valid
geltend: effective
gemacht: constructed
Gemüt: mind
geniessen: to enjoy
Genuss: enjoyment
Glaube: faith
Glück: happiness
Glückseligkeit: Happiness (see note 7, p. 44 above)
gültig: valid
Gültigkeit: validity
Handlung: action
hervorbringen: to produce
das Ich: the ego
letzter Zweck: ultimate purpose
Lust: pleasure
Materie: matter
mittelbar: indirect
Objekt: object
Prüfung: examination
Recht (recht): right
Religiosität: religiousness
Schicksale: fortunes
schliessen: to infer
Schluss: inference
Sein: being
Selbsttätigkeit: self-activity
Seligkeit: blessedness
setzen: to posit
Sinnenempfindung: sensation
Sinnenwelt: sensuous world *or* world of sense
sinnlich: sensuous

Sinnlichkeit: sensibility
Spontaneität: spontaneity
Stoff: material
Trieb: impulse
übersinnlich: supersensuous
unmittelbar: direct *or* immediate
Vergnügen: enjoyment
Vernunft: reason
Verstand: understanding

Vorstellung: representation
Wesen: (a) being *or* essence
Wille: will
Willkür: choice
wirkende Ursache: efficient cause
Wollen: volition
zufällig: contingent
Zweck: purpose
zweckmässig: purposive

Select Bibliography

I. GERMAN EDITIONS OF FICHTE'S WORKS

[Fichte, Johann Gottlieb.] *Versuch einer Critik aller Offenbarung*. Königsberg: Im Verlag der Hartungschen Buchhandlung, 1792.

Fichte, Johann Gottlieb. *Versuch einer Kritik aller Offenbarung*. Zweite, vermehrte, und verbesserte Auflage. Königsberg: Im Verlag der Hartungschen Buchhandlung, 1793.

Johann Gottlieb Fichte's sämmtliche Werke. Edited by I. H. Fichte. 8 vols. Berlin: Verlag von Veit & Comp., 1845–6. Reprint edition. Berlin: Walter de Gruyter & Co., 1971.

Fichte, Johann Gottlieb. *Werke: Auswahl in sechs Bänden*. Edited by Fritz Medicus. Leipzig: Fritz Eckardt Verlag, 1911.

J. G. Fichte-Gesamtausgabe der Bayerischen Akademie der Wissenschaften. Edited by Reinhard Lauth and Hans Jacob. Stuttgart-Bad Cannstatt: Friedrich Frommann Verlag (Günther Holzboog), 1962ff.

II. ENGLISH TRANSLATIONS OF FICHTE'S WORKS

A complete annotated bibliography of English translations of Fichte's writings, by Daniel Breazeale, appears in *Idealistic Studies* 6 (September 1976), pp. 280–5.

The Popular Works of Johann Gottlieb Fichte. Translated by William Smith. 2 vols. London: J. Chapman, 1848–9. 4th ed., rev., London: Trübner & Co., 1889. Vol. 2 includes *The Way Towards the Blessed Life, or The Doctrine of Religion*.

The Science of Knowledge. Translated by A. E. Kroeger. Philadelphia: J. B. Lippincott, 1869. Reprint ed. London: Routledge & Kegan ing 'The Religious Significance of the Science of Knowledge.'

The Science of Rights. Translated by A. E. Kroeger. Philadelphia: J. B. Lippincott, 1869. Reprint ed. London: Routledge & Kegan Paul, 1970.

The Science of Ethics as Based on the Science of Knowledge. Translated by A. E. Kroeger. Edited by W. T. Harris. London: Kegan Paul, Trench, Trübner & Co., 1897.

Addresses to the German Nation. Translated by R. F. Jones and
G. H. Turnbull, Chicago: Open Court, 1922. Edited and revised by
George Armstrong Kelly. New York: Harper & Row, 1968.

The Vocation of Man. Edited by Roderick M. Chisholm. The Library of
Liberal Arts, vol. 50. Indianapolis: Bobbs-Merrill Co., 1956. The
translation is a revision of the one by William Smith.

'On the Foundation of Our Belief in a Divine Government of the
Universe.' Translated by Paul Edwards. In *19th Century Philosophy.*
Edited by Patrick L. Gardiner. New York: The Free Press, 1969.
Pp. 19–26.

*Science of Knowledge (Wissenschaftslehre), with the First and Second
Introductions.* Edited and translated by Peter Heath and John
Lachs. New York: Appleton-Century-Crofts, 1970.

III. SECONDARY LITERATURE

Copleston, Frederick. *A History of Philosophy.* Vol. 7, *Fichte to
Nietzsche.* London: Burns and Oates, 1963.

Gogarten, Friedrich. *Fichte als religiöser Denker.* Jena: Eugen Diederichs,
1914.

Gurwitsch, Georg. *Fichtes System der konkreten Ethik.* Tübingen:
J. C. B. Mohr, 1924.

Hartmann, Nicolai. *Geschichte des deutschen Idealismus.* 2nd ed.
2 vols. in 1. Berlin: Walter de Gruyter & Co., 1960.

Henrich, Dieter. *Fichtes ursprüngliche Einsicht.* Frankfurt: Kloster-
mann, 1967.

Hirsch, Emanuel. *Fichtes Religionsphilosophie im Rahmen der philo-
sophischen Gesamtentwicklung Fichtes.* Göttingen: Vandenhoeck &
Ruprecht, 1914.

*Geschichte der neuern evangelischen Theologie, im Zusammenhang
mit den allgemeinen Bewegungen des europäischen Denkens.*
Vol. 4. Gütersloh: C. Bertelsmann Verlag, 1951.

Kroner, Richard. *Von Kant bis Hegel.* 2 vols. in 1. Tübingen: J. C. B.
Mohr (Paul Siebeck), 1961.

Ritzel, Wolfgang. *Fichtes Religionsphilosophie.* Stuttgart: W. Kohlhammer Verlag, 1956.

Sieber, Fritz. *Weltanschauung und Offenbarung beim jungen Fichte.*
Berlin: Verlag des Evangelischen Bundes, 1940.

Wagner, Falk. *Der Gedanke der Persönlichkeit Gottes bei Fichte und
Hegel.* Gütersloh: Verlagshaus Gerd Mohn, 1971.

Index

alienation, 10–11, 27–8, 73
Allgemeine Literatur-Zeitung, 5
asceticism, 138n
atheism controversy, 22–3
Attempt at a Critique of all Revelation
composition and publication of, 3–6
summary of contents, 6–14
attention, 14, 109, 111–13, 121–2, 124–5

belief, 9, 62
see also faith
blessedness, 59, 174

categories, 129, 135, 146–7, 157–61
cause
and effect, 120–1, 138, 150
efficient, 86, 88–9
final, 86, 88–9
Christianity, 15, 22, 24, 29, 80, 142n, 172
cognition, faculty of, 100–1, 129
Columbus, Christopher, 121–2n
critical (Kantian) philosophy, viii, 2, 20, 54, 58, 79–80, 93n

Deists, 25–6, 27, 28
see also Tindal, Matthew
desire, faculty of, 40, 46–7, 49, 55, 63–6, 103, 152–3, 156–8, 164n, 165, 168–9, 173
higher, 47, 52, 57, 59, 63, 69, 72, 100–1, 118–19, 128, 153–4, 156n, 157, 168
lower, 45, 59, 63, 100–1, 152, 153–4, 157, 168

determinism, 2, 20–1
dogmatics, 134–5
duty, 22, 57, 68, 85, 101, 106–7, 116, 128, 136, 138, 139, 159, 175–6
conflict of inclination and, 72, 74, 103, 154

ego (*das Ich*), 21–2, 24, 49, 143
Enlightenment, 22, 24–6

faith, 9, 27, 130, 131, 134, 157n
in revelation, 157–61, 164n, 168–72
see also belief
Feuerbach, Ludwig, 27–8
freedom
causality through, 84, 120–2, 176
of choice, 52–4
of conscience, 171
vs. necessity, 20–1, 24, 45, 46, 60–1, 118–19
presupposed in morality, 8, 15, 102, 107–8, 114–17, 125, 128–9, 134–5, 137, 140, 158

God
as author of revelation, 85–7, 108–11, 121, 137, 138, 148, 151
authority of, 11, 109, 111, 113–14, 124, 130, 132
concept of, 9, 12, 21–2, 24, 27–8, 60–3, 70, 89, 93, 124, 128, 140–3, 146, 149, 152–3, 155, 158, 174
as creator, 11, 77–8, 103, 107
as executor of moral law, 11, 62–3, 68–9, 76, 101, 119–20
existence of, 8–9, 23, 55n, 60,

nature – *cont.*
  vs. morality, 8, 24, 61, 68–9

orthodoxy, rational, 27

pantheism, 23
Paul, Saint, 144n
permission, 56, 60, 71, 136, 156n
persecution, 125, 133
pleasant, 41–4, 55, 56, 104
pleasure and displeasure, feeling of,
  64–5
positivity, 16–17, 28–9
prayer, 136, 138n
probability, 150–1
prophecy, 130
purpose, concept of, 84, 86–7, 146–7
purposiveness, 64, 66, 77

reason
  postulates of, 7–10, 13, 57, 58, 61,
    74, 80, 86, 91, 95, 118, 119,
    128, 130n, 131, 134, 140, 157n
  practical, 8, 13, 19–21, 24, 25, 29,
    39, 45, 67–8, 71–2, 74–5, 76–7,
    91, 98, 110, 114, 119, 129, 131–
    4, 138, 143, 147, 149, 152,
    155, 157n, 162, 170, 175
  theoretical, 8, 20–1, 24, 67–8, 75,
    76, 91, 110, 121, 128–30, 138,
    152, 163, 173
  see also Kant, Immanuel, *Critique
    of Practical Reason*, *Critique of
    Pure Reason*
receptivity, 40, 48
Reinhard, Franz Volkmar, 35
Reinhold, K. L., 6
religion
  concept of, 8–12, 76–81, 82, 90,
    135
  deduction of, 60–75, 162
  in modern thought, 26–8
  natural (rational), 11–12, 23, 25–6,
    79–80, 100–3, 108, 109, 116–
    17, 122n, 134, 160–1
  philosophy of, in Kant and Fichte,
    15–18
  purpose of, 170–1

revealed, 25–6, 79–81, 100–17,
  125, 147
universality of, 165
in *Wissenschaftslehre*, 20, 22–3
see also Deists
respect, feeling of, 48–52, 55, 72–3,
  129, 137
resurrection, 144
see also immortality
revelation
  concept of, 12, 39, 162
    formal, 82–90
    material, 91–4
  criteria of, 14, 97, 99, 123–47, 151,
    153, 155, 160, 163
  critique of (program), 12, 39, 97–9,
    162–4
  deduction of, 13–14, 92–3, 95–9
  empirical need for, 92–3, 97–8,
    100–17, 118, 123–4, 127, 159,
    163
  function of, 114–15
  importance of, in modern thought,
    25–30
  see also religion, revealed
right, concept of, 47, 52, 54, 56–7, 59,
  60, 63–9, 76, 95, 97, 117, 161

Schelling, F. W. J. von, 2
Schleiermacher, F. D. E., 23, 27
Schultz, Johann, 3, 4
self-activity, 40, 41, 45, 47, 54, 60
  see also spontaneity
sensation, 40–4, 46, 52, 83, 116
  faculty of, 48, 76
sensibility, 51n, 56, 80, 82, 104–8,
  116–17, 118, 136, 138n, 139–45
sin, 15–16
Spinoza, Benedict, 2
spontaneity, 40, 42, 44, 45, 46, 47–8,
  52–3, 54, 89, 116
  see also self-activity
Stäudlin, Carl Friedrich, 37n
sublime, feeling of, 51n

theology, 10–11, 12, 26–7, 63, 65,
  67, 76
  see also dogmatics